UNEXPECTED
WISDOM

UNEXPECTED
WISDOM

*Major Insight from
the Minor Prophets*

DAN SCHMIDT

Baker Books
A Division of Baker Book House Co
Grand Rapids, Michigan 49516

© 2002 by Dan Schmidt

Published by Baker Books
a division of Baker Book House Company
P.O. Box 6287, Grand Rapids, MI 49516-6287

Printed in the United States of America

Library of Congress Cataloging-in-Publication Data

Schmidt, Dan, 1957–
    Unexpected wisdom : major insight from the Minor Prophets / Dan Schmidt.
      p.   cm.
    Includes bibliographical references.
    ISBN 0-8010-6379-5 (pbk.)
    1. Bible. O.T. Minor Prophets—Criticism, interpretation, etc. I. Title.
BS1560.S33 2001
224′.906—dc21
                                             2001043269

For current information about all releases from Baker Book House, visit our web site: http://www.bakerbooks.com

To
Mom and Dad——on both sides——
whose wise counsel flowered fully
because it was so deeply rooted

CONTENTS

Introduction   9

1 **Receive and Extend Grace**   15
  Jonah
2 **Don't Fear the Dark**   30
  Habakkuk
3 **Abandon Pride**   44
  Obadiah
4 **Use Power Well**   60
  Micah
5 **Choose Wisely**   75
  Haggai
6 **Be Courageous**   92
  Amos
7 **Stay Close**   111
  Hosea
8 **Keep Your Heart Soft**   126
  Joel
9 **Radiate Integrity**   140
  Malachi
10 **Hope**   154
  Nahum, Zephaniah, and Zechariah

Notes   170

Introduction

here is a closet in your house, packed full. Occasionally, you reach inside for an item you want or need. Each time there is more in this small room than you remember. And more than you know is hidden there.

One day you open the door wide as you search out a particular thing. You switch on the light and are astonished at how much has accumulated on the shelves. You slide back a suit bag, recalling why you bought what is tightly zipped inside. Behind the clothes, amid the jumble of sports gear and baby toys, a box catches your eye. You pull off its top and riffle through the photos and papers stored within. Where did this come from? you wonder. Oh, I remember that! you exult. You slide to the floor, musing, your earlier search waylaid by this new discovery.

We move through days packed to the brim. We do our best on the paths before us: Some are murky, others clear, most challenge. Media clamor for our attention, hawking navigational aids. Many—even people of faith—buy in.

The search for assistance is serious business, the quest of one's life. So where will we go? With whom will we consult?

People of faith—followers of Jesus—have the Bible, that book packed full as a closet. Some parts of this Bible are well known, accessible, and often perused: history, gospel, epistle. Other bits are less so, like those pesky genealogical tables. Or the Minor Prophets.

Minor Prophets? Exactly. Those books wedged between the "Major" Prophets (such as Isaiah and Jeremiah) and Matthew. What if you step in, push through the familiar, reach down, and peel back the cover from them—what treasure might emerge? There are mysteries here for sure, along with rich delights. These Prophets demand, and they intrigue.

The prophets denounce ancient sins. They plead for whole-hearted devotion. Like no other group, prophets emanate a holy dissatisfaction with the status quo. They look at what they see and can't stand it: The days of our lives are too empty, they say, the passion of our hearts too tepid, the focus of our intentions too diffuse. They demand a reckoning.

The day of reckoning is one of those prominent prophetic themes, but before this climactic accounting there are many seasons of taking stock. The prophets simply want all God's people to be fully devoted to him. Of course, this does not mean that the Minor Prophets make for an easy read. They plead for depth, and heeding that call requires effort, much as securing a degree requires effort, or raising a child, or sculpting.

Going Down Deep

East of the Continental Shelf, just beyond the Bahamas, the floor of the Atlantic Ocean plunges. If after breakfast you board a cabin cruiser at Nassau's harbor and head full throttle through the Northeast Providence Channel, you'll be in deep seas by lunch. The water's color changes as you pound over it, summoning hues from the *big* box of crayons: robin's egg, aqua, turquoise, blizzard, cornflower, midnight. Cut back the engines and bob on the swells. Now slip on a mask and fins. Shrug the scuba pack on to your back. Step off the stern platform.

You're impressed immediately by what you encounter. You won't see the bottom any time soon; you won't see much after an hour heading down. In fact, long after you lose light from the surface, you will still be far from the ocean floor. Submersed in this ocean, you are very small.

It may feel as though you've left all that is real only to tumble into a realm where there is no way to orient yourself. You sink, sucked downward by gravity—alone, forgotten, destined to perish. And along the way, it's dark.

Many view life with God in similar terms. To be a person for whom God is real and significant, they assume, requires a headlong plunge into an unenlightened life that eventually ends in a choked gasp. It is much easier, more real even, to bob in a boat on the surface.

To sink into God? What is that all about? Won't the trip be unsettling? Won't the pressure of life near God overwhelm? Or might it be—just maybe—that exchanging what I know for a life infused by God may be a good deal? Mysterious, puzzling, dark—yes, at times. But also powerful, dynamic, deep. To such a life, the prophets beckon.

Messengers of God

Prophets are to society what Allied planes were to the P.O.W. camps, what radio broadcasts were behind the Iron Curtain, what fax traffic was to China in the days of Tiananmen Square: They are the beacons of—the beckoners to—what is still to come. At times the prophets pound people for misbehavior and aberrant attitudes, but they also hold out hope.

First, they see who God is and what he is up to, and then they come with a message. They stand and they preach in the face of withering criticism and stifling apathy and physical torment because they have no choice. The God who has swept them off their feet in a gale has taken them out to sea and plunged them down deep. They come up for air, or take a trip back to the mainland, with a message from the same God, who comes and who cares.

"Our God comes and will not be silent," a poet said (Ps. 50:3). He might have been describing prophets, because God grasps these most human of people to raise the hue and cry, "Things are not as they should be! Get right or be left!" The writings of prophets occupy more space than any other genre in Scripture; the sheer weight of their witness should tell us that God loves to show himself and that he has a great deal to say. The frequency of prophetic utterance is another proof that God is not aloof—a little difficult to understand and accept at times, but not absent. He sends prophets, fills them, makes himself known through them.

When God has something to say, he takes hold of a prophet. So says Amos (3:7), who gives us insight into this line of work. For Amos, as for the others, God is One whose voice cannot be ignored. He speaks often, and when he does, there is no recourse but to get up, go out, and deliver the message. God plucks prophets from the temple, the orchard, and the marketplace, fuses his terrible love into their hearts, and sets them loose in the henhouse. Feathers fly.

The Message of the Minors

The Minor Prophets[1] defy easy categorization. Of the twelve books, about half include specifics about time and location; the other half are variously placed by scholars early or late, north or south, written by people known or obscure. The books are short and long, prose and poetry.

A friend asked, when I told him of my interest in the Minors, whether I thought any of them didn't belong. He was joking, and I bobbled a snappy comeback. As I think about it now, I conclude that none of them belong; each Minor Prophet was a misfit.

Maybe that's why these prophets tend to be grouped together; maybe that's why they get pushed from view. Time was, prophecy captivated congregations. These days, the Prophets are less known, and the Minors typically make appearances only during Advent or tithing appeals. Few know much anymore about the preaching of Zephaniah or Habakkuk.

They deserve better. Though short, these books are hardly minor. As Goliath discovered that fateful day, size is relative.

My interest in the Minor Prophets has been fueled by sermons, classes, casual reading, and close study. Experience too, from a decade of pastoring in Maryland, when our church bravely embraced the prospect of becoming pure and winsome followers of Christ. We realized how much we needed to chip away at hearts hardened to grace; we were given opportunities to show mercy; we found our faith scrutinized and stretched; we longed for better days. In short, we were living the Minor Prophets.

This book is an attempt to pull back and look at the life Minor Prophets advocate, to grapple with an incisive biblical commentary on the life we're after. With this devotional exegesis, I am envisioning two kinds of readers, both represented by friends over the years. One is the seasoned churchgoer, who views the Old Testament in terms of boredom (brought on by too many Sunday school classes on too few topics) and/or guilt (The speaker who leans over the pulpit only to accuse, "When was the last time you read Leviticus?" sticks vividly in the memory). My hope is to highlight writers and books that are perhaps unfamiliar and yet wonderfully apt, and then engage with them in a constructive dialogue.

Another reader is the new adult convert who, coming to things Christian, often picks up the Old Testament. Ironically, what tends to bore those raised on an endless Sunday school litany of creation, Noah, and Saul tends to fascinate those who come to the text later in life with adult experiences and concerns. For these disciples, I hope to present the Minors as writings also worth attention. Pastors and laypeople alike come from both groups, and this book addresses some particular concerns of those actively engaged in local church ministry.

The Minor Prophets provide a portal, not only to viewing the Old Testament in fresh ways, but for walking through to the life gone deep into God. These books confront readers with powerful, recurring themes; they bring us directly into the arena with God so that we can grapple with our ideas about him. With these prophets we reexamine, individually and corporately, matters essential for spiritual development: grace, faith, mercy, discipline. The Minors challenge our approach to life, our interaction with others.

As I was entering pastoral ministry, I had some conversations with my father, an experienced churchman. An observation of his about sermons stuck with me. "The challenge for preachers," he suggested, "is to figure out what not to say. After all the study they pour into a topic, it must be very easy to want to share everything they've learned each week."

He's right: It is. So the wise preacher must distill. I approached this book with the same mind-set. The more I probe the Minor Prophets, the more I find, but to keep the size of this book manageable, I've tried to limit the scope of each chapter to one or two ideas from each prophet. That's difficult, because they are so rich. But it will be enough if these chapters whet appetites for further study and consideration.

The Minor Prophets' message is to go down deep. From the safety of shore or even the relative security of a large boat, that big step always looks scary. But the promise is that as people step out, God is waiting. They can, therefore, take the plunge. As Paul says (to paraphrase 2 Cor. 4:8), this journey with and toward God is fraught with difficulty; people who make it will experience enormous pressure. But because God is there, they will never be crushed.

The Minors catch us unawares, almost in between our search for something else, with a message seekers like us need. Finding it among them may surprise us, the way a bargain hunter is surprised to discover behind a garage sale velvet Elvis a previously unknown van Gogh. But we do well to notice their unmistakable value: These Prophets would make us wise to the ways of God.

1

RECEIVE AND EXTEND GRACE

Jonah

*J*onah was swallowed by a whale. Every kid who has ever put in time at Sunday school knows this. Even those unfamiliar with Sunday school could, in all likelihood, complete the phrase "Jonah and the _____." Like Noah and the _____, Jonah's tale has seeped into our culture, one of the handful of stories many could class as "biblical."

So the basic elements of the tale are known: There's Jonah; there's a whale. So what? Exactly. A story as "familiar" as Jonah and the whale is bound to suffer. Some aspects get amplified, others are forgotten, and the book gets flattened into a two-dimensional flannelgraph. In this way, the radical nature of Jonah is lost.

The Book of Jonah is radical for two reasons. First, because it deals with core ("radical" comes from the Latin *radix*, for "root") issues such as forgiveness, motivation, and grace. Second, because it shakes so many preconceived ideas about how things ought to work. Take the opening lines: God speaks to Jonah, and then Jonah runs away. Do we expect this? Of course not! We expect that when God speaks, people listen and obey. What we get instead is a prophet—a *prophet,* no less!—ignoring divine revelation.

God Speaks and People Respond

Each book in the Minors begins with some affirmation of God's communication. We easily miss this, because we are accustomed to ignoring the first bit of something: We fast-forward through a video's opening credits, we tear off the cereal box top, disregarding its colorful text, we skip a book's introduction. We are eager for the heart of the matter, to discover what's inside, or still ahead. In the case of the Minors, if we use that sort of approach we will blow right by a fundamental point with which each book begins: God is speaking, and we need to listen. We can hear the scrape of the storm door when it opens the morning after we've called for overnight delivery of an urgently desired computer part or stereo component, but do we hear God?

When God speaks, it is to people: He speaks personally, and so we should take it personally. His Word should bore into our hearts, working its way down deep to surround and permeate our life. It is, however, frightfully easy to resist. We doze through sermons, compose grocery lists during prayer meetings, swat flies during "quiet times." We seize on reports of religious experiences without pausing for critical reflection; we let excesses pass and rationalize absences. We substitute many words for the Word.

The prophets bring God's Word and call people to take the message to heart such that their lives exude the truth and beauty of that Word. In our day, God speaks most frequently and obviously in the Bible, and so we read carefully, listening attentively for his voice. We discover there that at one point God's Word took on flesh (John 1:14), and in this incarnation, the Word was delivered in new and powerful ways. A while later, this incarnated Word left, and in his place, the Spirit came.

When Jesus, the God-man who personified the Word, spoke about this Spirit, he said that the Spirit would guide, remind, and teach (John 14 and 16 give us some of Jesus' words on the Spirit). Through the Spirit, God continues to speak. This keeps the Word alive and active (Heb. 4:12), and in some respects, even new.[1]

These words from God have weight and purpose. Most often in the prophets, they challenge behavior and attitude, appealing for a change in people who are straying from him. Assurance of presence, promise of assistance, and the threat of punishment round out the set of prophetic words—but all are directed at prompting life changes, all encourage a response. As Amos says so eloquently, when the lion roars, people jump (Amos 3:8).

Jonah is an obvious example. When the Word of the Lord comes to Jonah, he hears and understands. How does he change? He runs away. Why? Jonah's response was probably the result of several factors, such as fear, stubbornness, and a sense of offense. To "preach against Nineveh" (1:2) was to travel as God's emissary to an establishment known for cruelty and barbarism with the news of God's concern. Not only was this dangerous (Jeremiah gives voice to the dilemma from the forge of his own experience in Jer. 20:8), but it was also distasteful: Could God be serious about wanting these violent pagans to hear the gospel?

Rationally, Jonah could agree with God's description of himself—"I knew that you are a gracious and compassionate God, slow to anger and abounding in love, a God who relents from sending calamity"—but the conclusion was still upsetting: "That is why I was so quick to flee to Tarshish" (4:2). He cannot bring himself to endorse a good outcome for Nineveh, and so in response to a personal word that he clearly understands, Jonah bolts.

We expect a prophet's response to be more like this: "When your words came, I ate them; they were my joy and my heart's delight" (Jer. 15:16). Jonah shows a distinctly human tendency: God speaks and Jonah ignores him, even runs the other way. Instead of holiness, we get the most natural response, and we nearly laugh from sheer pity. Or we take umbrage. Why do we who so often struggle with faith and obedience need to hear the tale of one who doesn't really, well, succeed? For two reasons.

First, the very presence of this story in Scripture argues for its—and, more broadly, the Bible's—authenticity. By retaining so unflattering a story, the Bible hardly comes across as a fabricated document meant to dupe and mislead. Second, Jonah's story is one we need, precisely because we are people who struggle with faith and obedience.

God's Word comes inexorably, like waves rolling onto the beach, sometimes gently, sometimes like a tsunami. And when it comes, responses vary. We might listen, comprehend, and act accordingly, taking from these words the sweet nourishment that Jeremiah found. Or we might take off, like Jonah.

We run for different reasons: Our sense of justice is offended, or we are scared by the implications, or we are immersed in our own pursuits, or we are ornery. We might conclude, having heard God speak, that the word he delivers, the acts he commends, the behavior he restricts, the jobs he offers—none of these has any appeal. So we tinker with our own interests instead, like the little child on the kitchen floor, oblivious to her mother's entreaties. Finally, in desperation, Mom takes the kid to the doctor for a hearing test. The results are positive: Her hearing is fine. The problem lies with her desire to listen and to obey. To obey means submitting one will to another, and at times, to engage in activity that is different, or unpleasant, or strange, or dangerous. To listen and obey takes me outside myself, away from my own direction and into the realm of another. I relinquish control over my own destiny when I let another's words direct me. I am no longer my own master.

To assert that I am, in fact, the captain of my own destiny, I must prove the point. So I stand and chart a course by my own lights. I will go to Tarshish. This Jonah does, resolute in his resistance to the Word. But on the passage, a storm comes, brought on by the divine gift of a strong wind (1:4). This wind is enough to terrify seasoned watermen, who proceed to follow the only course they know. They lift their prayers and heave their cargo, hoping that one or the other will produce good results. Neither works, of course, and it is only when the captain rouses[2] the one person who might solve their problem that a solution is discovered. It comes when Jonah draws the short straw and asks to be thrown overboard.

The sailors, to their credit, think more highly of Jonah's God than that (1:9–10). They attempt to improve their situation without resorting to human sacrifice, but ultimately, reluctantly, they pitch Jonah into the sea (1:13–15). Instantly, the waves recede and Jonah disappears. The sailors speed away, awestruck.

A Message of Grace

Jonah is left behind but not alone. As you know, he is swallowed by a "great fish" (1:17). What sort of fish? As a kid, I imagined Jonah to be an ancient Pinocchio, from the Disney cartoon, wandering aimlessly in the cavernous innards of an enormous whale. But the text is not plain: While "great fish" could mean "whale," about the only firm data we have is that whatever was big enough to take Jonah whole was also small enough to deposit him on or near shore (see 2:10). Perhaps it was a killer whale that swallowed the prophet, the thirty-foot variety you see on the nature channel that beaches itself in search of seals. Or maybe it was something even a little smaller.

I grew up in the Bahamas and spent a great deal of time on the water. Once while boating, we pulled up near a small cay, where the water was shallow. We drifted along lazily, and I happened to glance over one side. There, swimming next to us, was a shark.

The first shark I saw as a kid nearly killed me—not from mangling but from fear. After that episode, I learned to distinguish "bad" sharks (such as hammerheads, which are born mean and ugly) from "good" sharks (such as nurse sharks, which are common and curious but only dangerous if their rough skin rubs you the wrong way). The shark I saw while in the boat was a nurse shark—no big deal. What did impress me, however, was its size. I was in a fifteen-foot boat, and this shark's nose and tail passed either end. I was also impressed when I realized that this shark had come with a friend and that our boat was flanked by a pair of the enormous creatures.

As I said, these were "good" sharks, so I wasn't worried. But I was also glad to be in the boat. And there we drifted, in less than four feet of water, about a hundred yards offshore. Could a man have fit in either of these sharks? Probably. Could he have made it to dry land from the belly of such a fish? Easily.

The second chapter of Jonah gives us the prophet's epiphanal prayer inside the fish. Maybe that prayer came from a man free to roam, but I think more likely that it grew in one whose movements were restricted, who was left with little more space than he needed to collect his thoughts.

Whatever the circumstance, this much is clear: Jonah, from inside the fish, offers one mighty prayer. It is a revelation of self-perception, a recognition of life's fleeting nature. The prophet understands that things are bad not only because he is far from any known place and tangled in the guts of a sea monster, but also because he is falling farther from God.

This realization draws the prophet back to his senses. He knows, for example, that despite desperate conditions, God has not abandoned him ("You listened" [2:2]). He is confident that although life is nearly over, God can restore him ("You brought my life up" [2:6]). He believes that in such a time, seeking God is essential ("My prayer rose" [2:7]).

That prayer indicates a thawing of Jonah's heart. For the first time, he acknowledges God's grace (2:8); for the first time he appears open to hearing and obeying God by making good on his vow (2:9). In this prayer, Jonah finally sounds like a prophet as he keys in on the problem of idolatry, since prophets regularly denounced the corrupting influence of idols that was splintering their nation.

Idolatry is not simply an ancient problem, of course; we regularly find ways to fashion substitute deities in a modern age. Any time we make sacrifices to—or for—something other than God, we are victims of idolatry. Any who fall under its sway forfeit grace, which, according to Jonah, is otherwise ready to fall on them.

Idolaters make the fatal error of thinking that they are capable of providing what only grace can supply. The sailors collected gods, including Jonah's, like seashells, without any further commitment.

The Ninevites, proud and arrogant (see Zeph. 2:15), raised their prowess as an idol. Even Jonah, the self-serving prophet, is an idolater, for he follows his own course rather than that of God. All risk the forfeiture of God's grace because of their idolatry.

And yet, Jonah's prayer holds out hope. Grace is resisted only to the point that people cling to idols. Should they release their grip, what happens then? If a person "lets go and lets God," will grace come? Yes. That is the message of this little book. Grace comes, even to one like Jonah, who can be a prophet of impact (see 2 Kings 14:25), as well as a dolt, clinging to bad messages.

Does his reluctance to obey remove him from God's grace? Will Nineveh's grisly past effectively exempt them from grace? No. And this is the message of the book too. As humility replaces the arrogance of idolatry, grace can finally fall. Even on Nineveh. Even on Jonah. God will go to great lengths to see this happen and is not above using extraordinary measures to show or shower grace.

The prayer inside that fish should have exposed Jonah to the grace capable of changing him. With his soul at full ebb, surrounded by vivid indicators of personal rebellion and faced with a God still wanting to show him grace, Jonah should have been gloriously reoriented in the cell of prayer, ready to burst out with fresh vigor. His opportunity comes when the fish spits him out and again the Lord speaks (3:1–2). With this, God shows that a relationship with him is not like a sheet of glass that once dropped is forever splintered into a myriad of pieces. Repair—restoration—is possible; grace grants a fresh start.

Jonah appears to have come under its influence, as he strides purposefully toward Nineveh and begins his preaching tour immediately. There, his words make an impact. The king of Nineveh declares, in a flurry of amazingly perceptive theological insight, the need for prayer, fasting, and repentance (3:7–9). The entire city immediately and decisively renounces their sin and turns to God. It's a miracle! Nowhere else does Scripture record so massive a revival.

The grace that could be the Ninevites' suddenly is, in an outpouring from God that should have brought Jonah to his knees in thanksgiving. Instead, the sincere response of previously godless people elicits anger over God's compassion; grace has left

Jonah curiously unmoved. The one thing Jonah does not want, God gives. This story is full of things God does, brings, and causes: a great wind (1:4), a great fish (1:17), a vine (4:6), a worm (4:7), another wind (4:8). The one time God stays his hand and does not bring the threatened destruction (3:10), Jonah is upset.

The surprise, of course, is that exactly the opposite of what we would expect occurs. We expect the prophet to move on down the road of grace, growing ever closer to God, while the wicked Ninevites slowly turn over a spit in hell. Instead, we learn that the pagans convert and that the prophet wanders off, muttering.

Our Need for Grace

We expect, because Jonah is in the Bible, and a prophet no less, that he will be, well, holier than we are. What we get is a guy who runs from God, curls up to sleep and avoid a world in uproar, makes an outlandish offer to sacrifice himself for others, and then winds up in a fish where he suddenly becomes religious. Oh yes. He also gets a second chance from God, but then when he complies, the results disappoint him and he heads out to sulk. By a person like this we're supposed to be inspired? Maybe God should just sweep him away and start over.

But he doesn't. Does God have no shame? Can't he find better servants?

I recall a long car ride with a friend who was struggling with faith. "I'd find it easier to become a Christian," my friend said, "if I didn't know so many Christians." By this my friend was saying that Christianity has obvious appeal, but many who live it are poor advertisements for it. Jonah is a case in point. He hardly seems a candidate for poster boy of the faith community.

The better question to ask is, *Why* does God let Jonah continue? When we ask that question, it isn't long before an answer starts to seep out: Jonah is a lot like us. In order for us to learn about grace, God is going to let us look in on Jonah's experience with it.

We might be inclined to think this book is about a whale. Or even about a wonderful conversion, of an entire city, no less. But when we focus on what we are reading, we discover that the book is really about Jonah and his need for conversion. And then we see: The book is really about us.

Think of the New Year's resolution you broke or the unkept promise you made to a child. What about that time you sat in a church service, stirred by the worship or the preacher's challenge; you made a pact with yourself—and God!—that you'd change, that you'd start something, or stop. But then . . .

We fall. We fail. We are not who we want to be as often as we'd like. Our good intentions are quickly framed and easily knocked over; we disappoint ourselves. Others disappoint us too. They make promises, offer assistance, assure us of imminent change— but then, they blow it. We live every day in a world desperately in need of grace.

Two Aspects of Grace

Our world needs grace. There is the grace that saves, which God brings, as he alone can save. There is also grace that shapes, grace that Jonah helps us understand, because of the way he fails to be formed by it. Jonah is called by God to deliver a message about the first aspect of grace, and he eventually does that. But when Jonah has opportunity to show what a life shaped by grace is like, he fails, miserably.

It is easy to think of needing grace the way I need my dad when I'm learning to ride a bike. He brings out that enormous two-wheeler for the first time and helps me climb on. He holds the seat and handlebars firmly as I tentatively crank the pedals. I wobble; he holds tight. I pick up speed; he starts to jog. I get my balance; he lets go. I'm riding now, and he's way back there, waving. I stand on the pedals and crank up the low hill. I turn at the top; it's iffy, but I don't fall. I coast down the hill, lifting one hand from the handlebars. I pass my dad, waving. He slowly turns and goes back to the house. I keep riding.

But the work of grace is not complete after a single, swift entrance. I have my life ahead of me still, and the very grace that saved me is the grace that I will need for every aspect of a life now made very different by the saving work of God. Grace now is the compressed air of the scuba diver who can explore caves and turn cartwheels underwater as long as that air keeps flowing. Remove the regulator and swim to the top on your own? Forget it. Your blood vessels will explode.

The problem is that we think we are on bikes and not strapped to an iron lung. We forget that the grace that brought us into God's presence is what keeps us functioning as we carry on with him. We try to move under our own power and then wonder about the cramps.

That puts us in the company of this prophet. We may be chosen by God and destined for a life with him, but so often we follow our whims and give place to idols: We pour ourselves out for work, pleasure, health, or goods. As a result, we live unevenly. The grace that saves us is supposed to be the grace that keeps us, the grace in which we are to grow (2 Peter 3:18). Too often we break away from his grip too soon, eager to ride alone. Then we find ourselves outside the city, brooding, letting our anger grow.

Grace Leads to Godliness

Anger seeps in when we resist grace. We might think it a sign of maturity (Don't older people get angry more often?) or a right in our society (I spent the money, went to school, paid my dues, worked all day, stayed up all night because of the baby, grew up with crummy parents . . .). We might pretend that we can manage it (holes in walls can be patched, bruises on faces heal, that smoldering in the stomach diminishes with a ten-mile run, or a trip to the mall, or chocolate).

But God is not amused. The Lord asks Jonah, "Have you any right to be angry?" (4:4, 9). "I do," he replies, and you can hear the pout. To this affirmation, God applies his standard: "Nineveh has more than a hundred and twenty thousand people who cannot tell their right hand from their left. . . . Should I not be concerned about that great city?" (4:11). His question goes unanswered, because the response is so obvious. Of course! Because God, it is in your nature to be concerned about the needy, whether they have physical or spiritual needs. That's who you are, that's what you do.

This answer puts a finger on our problem: We assume humanity exempts us from godliness. We take for granted that God will act graciously but then quickly excise grace from our own repertoire. Jonah's experience should convey a radically different idea, namely, that the grace God shows is precisely the grace people can show, precisely because God shows it. Grace is not only accessible and available; it is also pervasive and contagious. It fills and flows from God and should, therefore, be characteristic of those who belong to God.

One friend is part of a ministry couple who serves a number of churches in different countries. She moved to South America from a ranch where her family lived in a sprawling house they had designed themselves into a small apartment deep in town. My friend suffers from headaches frequently; she recently bid farewell to a child who traveled back to the United States for work and school.

My friend could easily complain; there is plenty about her life that is difficult or trying. She might even be justified in an occasional whine, and she is so often cheerful that others would quickly forgive or excuse a lapse. But she has never shown that side. Quite the opposite: She writes cards to me, my wife, and other friends, each one full of encouragement, each specific in calling attention to some detail worth commending. None ever concludes without drawing us closer to the Lord; grace oozes from her pen. Having seen her in a variety of settings, I have come to believe that if a scrap of bitterness even exists in her, it never gets sufficient attention to flourish.

This is because my friend is a saint. She takes seriously the impact of grace and has grown quite nicely into her sainthood. Sadly, I say this and risk misunderstanding. People might conclude that my friend is a rare bird, beautiful but elusive. In fact, every follower of Christ is called a saint (Eph. 1:1 offers just one example); it's just that we don't often think in those terms. It's like when we were children: Every kid is an artist, capable of drawing anything. But only a few stay with it as time passes, while the rest of us learn not to draw.

Do we view holiness similarly? God calls his people to holiness, and we experience what it's like for days, weeks, or years.

Then, for many of us, the thrill of such a life fades; we find that being a saint is a trifle tedious. We develop other interests; we learn not to draw. We substitute laws and fashion a list of rights: I have a right to free time, a right to be respected, a right to be heard, a right to be angry. Laws such as these, common as they are, separate us from each other and distance us from grace.

We meet people who stay artists, who relish being saints. Their holiness is evident and sometimes, frankly, mildly abrasive. "I could never be like *that*," we say. But is that right? Do we truly prefer what has crept in to replace the holiness once cherished—the anger, worry, fear? Is it a good idea to hold these things, to excuse them in ourselves, even to nurture their ongoing existence?

Anger makes us stupid. We lose track of how grace can dissipate anger. We lose confidence in the possibility of an unnatural response. We forget how delightful grace can make our life and that of others around us. The worm God sends (4:7) as Jonah sulks outside the city means that now the prophet will face the heat of God's grace that intends to melt anger. What the enormous fish helped provoke the tiny worm now continues. The bug's business exposes Jonah to the fullness of God (4:8), but once again the prophet seems to wrap around himself rather than succumb to grace (4:9).

Receive and Extend Grace

Once my father stopped for the light at a corner, and outside, on the sidewalk, my sister saw something fluttering. "Go get it," my mother urged me. So I bolted from the car, chased down the scrap of paper, and palmed it. Then I noticed it was a one-hundred-dollar bill. I returned to the open door, got in, and Dad drove off. The sheer surprise of this development brought a grin to each face. "You'll share that with your brother and sister, of course," my parents advised. "Of course," I agreed, all smiles.

Grace is like this: You don't expect a blessing of such magnitude to drop out of nowhere. Its inherent costliness makes us wary, and we can't easily accept that we might be the beneficiaries of such good fortune. We look around for someone, ready to hand it back, or to be asked for payment. Or we leave it lay, convinced that it's too good to be true and therefore must be false, or at least intended for someone else. There are many ways to miss the giddiness of grace.

Thankfully, there are occasions to receive grace too. We reach for what looks to be good and suddenly discover that it is—so good, in fact, that we can't believe our eyes. Will we take it home to keep? Will we dare to share our good fortune with another? Will we remember what the gift felt like, cherish that feeling, and allow our lives to change in order to accommodate that sensation? Will our lives be noticeably different, markedly improved, because of our association with grace?

God extends grace, and it is there for the taking. Idolatry can sway a person from grace, masking its beauty with a cheap substitute. But as grace breaks through and makes its impact, life is supposed to change. And part of that change involves extending grace once more. The recipients of grace are to be the announcers, demonstrators, and distributors of it. This is why God calls those "graced" to share the blessing they have received. It's a privilege far more than a duty (turning this sharing into a program diminishes the inherent winsomeness of grace) to reach out in this way, to "preach against Nineveh." We do it out of gratitude for having found what we did.

The net worth of my family increased that day through no industry of our own. We were simply in the right place at the right time; one saw, one encouraged, one ran, and all came away richer. Jonah, a man touched by God's grace, watched the balance sheet of an entire city's population soar, the result, at least in part, of his own willingness to share. But their newfound advantage left a sour taste in his mouth, and he could not find happiness in their newly acquired emancipation. The grace that saved him and them should have lined his heart with joy; instead, Jonah devised a way to remain bitter.

Grace Cannot Be Earned

It is a surprise that this book ends with Jonah still alive and angry.[3] Human instinct would have obliterated the prophet for his petulance. An editor committed to a happy ending would have tied the tale tight with Jonah's confession of hardness and sincere evidence of rehabilitation. Instead, God leaves Jonah with his life to live and a question to ponder. The answer to this question is as obvious as the completion to the simple phrase, "Jonah and the _____." Obvious, perhaps, but not simple.

We came to this book, expecting what we remembered from our youth: a rather straightforward, albeit fantastic, story about a guy and a whale. What we got was a new set of nagging questions: Why does God want Nineveh to hear the gospel? Why does God use a scoundrel like Jonah? Why doesn't Jonah get it?

Questions such as these reveal our bias. They show that our preference is for Scripture—God's Word—to be nice and neat, quaintly packaged, easy to unwrap, read, and set aside. What we get instead are surprises. It's like those cans that contain coiled springs. You open one innocently enough, but something quite unexpected leaps out.

Years ago, J. B. Phillips issued a warning: Your God is too small.[4] He was right. We read Jonah and think that the big player in the drama is a whale. What we find when we look closer is that God is the big one, expanding far beyond the space we give him. Grace is big too. We are not ready for this. We are fine with Jonah as a nice Sunday school worksheet or the answer to a Trivial Pursuit question. But a life-confronting situation disguised as a bedtime story? Hold on.

And this: While grace may be an unexpected theme, Jonah is certainly an unlikely hero. Once again, God breaks away from our preconceived ideas. This is because the notion of what ought to be acceptable to God is so fixed in our brains. We have such a difficult time believing that God could ever love a scoundrel like Jonah that he gives us a whole book simply to affirm that he does.

For God, grace is ready to fall on all who forego worthless idols, whether they be pagan Assyrians, esteemed Hebrew prophets, soccer moms, locksmiths, or diplomats. To restrict grace to the worthy is to miss the big idea of Scripture. This is what makes Jonah such an important book. Not only does Jonah announce the offer of grace to people who in no way deserve it, but the prophet goes on to prove that he himself is not even worthy of it.

Which is exactly the point: One does not earn grace. One simply stands under it like rain, allowing its cool refreshment to fill the dry cracks. And then one picks up a bucket and dumps it on someone else.

Grace flows from God not to those who earned it but on those who need it. This is why Jesus can mention Jonah with a straight face. Twice he recalls the prophet (Matt. 12:39–41; 16:4) as a way of describing his imminent death and resurrection. His appeal to Jonah says that God does not measure failure by human yardsticks. If he did, we'd all be sunk. Mercifully, God has a different standard. The thousands in Nineveh evoke his compassion not because they suddenly learned how to worship or tithe, or finally stopped smoking or beating their wives; they mattered because they existed, and because God is by nature full of grace.

It is easy to think that the book revolves around a single axle: Jonah being swallowed by a whale. It is more profitable to consider the book's parabolic slant. Its story worms its way into your life, nibbling at comfortable, nonpersonal exegesis. Parables are wonderfully suited for evoking this discomfort, and in this way, they regularly prompt constructive contemplation of God. Parables stir pots, raise questions, unsettle, stay with you. They keep you up with queries, or wake you with an "Aha!" but they do not go quietly into the night. Defined in this way, grace is parabolic too, because it will not leave you alone. And just when you think you have it figured out—bang!—the door flies open into a new room of enquiry.

Jonah was swallowed to be sure, but the fish was almost incidental. God overwhelms Jonah, encircles him, engulfs him in the vast arms of grace. There is no escaping the God of grace for this prophet. In the end, we don't know what happens with Jonah. Did he relent from his hardness? Repent of his stubbornness? Become a missionary pastor to Nineveh and live out the rest of his days there? We don't know, and for good reason. The book's final question keeps us from the smug appraisal that holds Jonah at a safe distance. We are meant to walk away scratching our heads, thinking about the conversions grace is supposed to bring.

2

DON'T FEAR
THE DARK
Habakkuk

Conversion. We toss this concept around like a football. "When did you convert?" we ask the seasoned missionary over dinner. "How many converts last year?" inquires the district supervisor as he reaches for the page of local church statistics. "Just tell us about your conversion," a worship leader instructs the advertising executive in preparation for a testimonial service. Conversion sounds like a simple change of plans, a matter of running into the end zone after a touchdown instead of kicking the ball through the uprights.

But conversion is more than a nudge at the top of a slide that sends us zooming down into God's arms. It's a journey, and there is friction along the way. Resistance comes from both external attacks by spiritual forces opposed to God and internal rebellion against his lordship. Strangely enough, there is also some turbulence from God.

This is because along the course of conversion, "we live by faith, not by sight" (2 Cor. 5:7). The faith by which we became converts is still necessary during the ongoing process of conversion that lasts throughout one's life with God. As Paul says in another letter, faith is "from first to last" (Rom. 1:17). It does not dissipate once a person enters God's kingdom, for conversion is not a one-time over and done event. Faith accompanies the convert throughout and will be nurtured by God along the way.

The nature of a convert's activity with respect to faith varies; often it resembles the program of an athlete engaged in weight training. Muscles need resistance to grow, and so an athlete must keep adding weight to the barbell and increasing the number of repetitions in order for muscle mass to increase. The fact that God would increase the resistance his people face surprises us at first: Shouldn't God try to make this new life on which they embark easier? What we find as we read Scripture, as we live the life he marks out, is that faith does not flourish very well in a five-star hotel. It develops far better when there are challenges and where it is dark.

James, for instance, links "trials of many kinds" with "the testing of your faith" (James 1:2–3). Peter explains the reason for this: Trials come so that faith "may be proved genuine and may result in praise, glory and honor" for God (1 Peter 1:7). Both James and Peter had firsthand experience with God's faith-training program, and each emerged with his faith intact and stronger. They wrote to encourage and to prepare converts for what was ahead. When God takes hold of your life, they would say, you can anticipate a secure future, and you can also be sure of a challenging present.

It is the latter that we watch unfold as we read Habakkuk, where we meet one who has converted to God's way. He is introduced as a prophet,[1] but that status does not exempt him from personal difficulty. Far from it. As we read we learn how God was active in helping Habakkuk's faith grow. His methods are startling. That is, they startle us because we are inclined to see things from Habakkuk's standpoint; we tend to think how gold must feel in the refiner's fire. When the heat increases, we pity the metal.

Step out of Habakkuk's sandals for a moment and view this situation from God's perspective. If you are committed to the increasing of faith, how will you help Habakkuk's faith grow? Remember, he is a prophet, accustomed to interacting often with God. He is familiar with the temple, a respected member of the community whose occupation places him often in a religious setting. He may well be spiritually advanced beyond many of his peers. He might be satisfied with the genuine progress he's already made. So how do you help his faith grow?

You press him; you lay on new weight. You plunge him into a setting he's never seen before. You take away the landmarks; you remove the familiar signs. You cast him adrift on an uncharted ocean and bring thick clouds in overhead. You want the faith of this convert to deepen, and that will happen only as the faith of this convert is challenged. So you push him into the dark, but you do not let go.

Personalized Growth

"Lord, don't you care if we drown?" The disciples, terrified by a sudden, ferocious storm, pounce on their sleeping Master. In a moment, Jesus is awake. Then he speaks: "Peace. Be still." At once the heaving water goes to glass. The power of Jesus captures our attention, but it is neither the only nor the main lesson. In each Gospel account, the context shows that Jesus has been circling the issue of faith. Mark's quartet of parables (chap. 4) revolving around the "seed" theme, Matthew's trio of miraculous healings (chap. 8), and Luke's duet of parables (chap. 8) all deal with faith. When the disciples finally face the furious storm, faith has come front and center.

"Where is your faith?" "Do you still have no faith?" "You of little faith, why are you so afraid?" Luke, Mark, and Matthew all mention Jesus' challenge as he presses the disciples for robust belief over blathering terror. For Jesus, fearing the storm is misguided. The real issue concerns faith, which is being tested—proven—by a storm.

The disciples were becoming accustomed to seeing a great deal: sick people getting well, lost people being taught. They themselves often saw Jesus up close and benefited from his special instruction. Now these disciples were embarking for another destination, to witness more teaching, another round of miracles. Could it be that they had fallen into a rut, expecting life to look a particular way?

A storm darkens the sky and slams into them, revealing their hearts. What's there? Fear, because they can no longer see very well. "Teacher, don't you care if we drown?" He does. But he is more interested in the focus and maturing of faith than in a consideration of death. For him, this storm is designed to develop faith.

The disciples do not catch this right away. I'm not sure I would have either. It is far more likely that, had I been in the boat, I would have been howling above the winds, racing across rain-slicked decks, tripping over cleats. I would have been the first one to grab Jesus' shoulder and shake him awake. "Don't you care if we drown?" Despite previous experience with the Lord, I panic when darkness sets in.

"You have so little faith," Jesus says to me. Yet, in his voice I hear a hint of possibility: My blurry faith may be small, but it is not nonexistent. It can grow. As the biblical record indicates, faith in God from the people of God is supposed to grow, and he is willing to go to great lengths to make sure that happens.

He selects what will be effective for the maturing of faith in particular hearts. For the disciples in the boat, it is a storm. For the temple prophet Habakkuk, it is an oracle—to start. God does not stop with this; there will be other ways of building faith.

This oracle from God (1:1) stirs up a nest full of questions clamoring like baby robins for attention. Habakkuk could have ignored the "destruction and violence" (1:3) around him, could have stayed by the temple gates, smiling and nodding as people walked in, oblivious or indifferent to what they said. Habakkuk might easily have opted for the idols preferred by so many, or honed his self-indulgence, or sunk into the pit of despair. He doesn't. He goes to God. But how strange: Apparently Habakkuk called several times and heard only silence from God (1:2).

Can God Be Trusted?

When a sailor sets out to circumnavigate the globe, he can anticipate both storms and doldrums. He will not be successful in accomplishing his goal unless he knows how to handle both, and so he will condition himself, outfit his craft, practice patience. When the squalls come, he will be ready, tuned. When his boat lays calm, he will not fret.

"How long, O LORD, must I call for help, but you do not listen?" (1:2). When the prophet observes how the ways of God, so dear to him, are held in low regard (1:2–4), he goes to God. He calls out. Nothing. He calls again. Silence. Habakkuk hits the doldrums. The disciples' faith was tested by furious winds and waves; the prophet sits becalmed. The voice of God so often present is not heard; it is a challenge for Habakkuk's faith.

We do not know how long Habakkuk waited. When God did eventually respond, what he says takes Habakkuk back into the realm of faith's testing once more. God sweeps all of the prophet's questions—"Why do you not save? Why do you make me look at injustice? Why do you tolerate wrong?" (1:2–3)—into a single basket and stuns Habakkuk: He promises action that involves the Babylonians. Once more, faith is on the line.

The Babylonians are some of Scripture's perennial villains. When an Old Testament prophet brings a message of denunciation, Babylon is often included in the list of "to be judged." Babylon is the sump of the Middle East, the low point into which other problems drain. Even in the New Testament, when John reaches for an image to encompass all that is opposed to God, he chooses Babylon (Revelation 18). So for God to suggest that Babylon will somehow be part of his plan makes us wonder about God. Can we trust a God like this?

The "testing" and "proving" of faith puts this question where we cannot miss it, because converts need to expand their conception of God. We slip into thinking that profound truths about God are easily grasped and that deep matters of the spirit are quickly accessed. We succumb to the notion that life with God can be expressed in terms that fit on a bumper sticker, or T-shirt, or CD insert. We assume God to be predictable, and so we take liberties with him. We forget that while he is personal, he is not pocket-sized. He is the one who holds a universe in his hands, and even the "God who hides himself" (Isa. 45:15). With the maturing of faith, our understanding of God will improve.

"I am raising up the Babylonians" (1:6). Anyone other than God asserting this would have made the prophet laugh out loud. The Babylonians? Those bloodthirsty, rapacious, no-account pagans? Why, the Babylonians were no better than the Assyrians, whose kingdom they were replacing. How could God even think about something constructive with *them*?

Years earlier, Jonah had been told to deliver good news to Nineveh, the Assyrian capital. Now, another prophet is brought into the counsel of God where he learns that Babylon, the current world power, is about to figure in God's plan as well. How do you count on a God who expects to use Babylonians? He pulls people away from safe harbor and sends them out to sea where anything could happen. A storm could blow in; the wind might die down.

The Babylonians. God is forever doing this: He fails to be predictable. He puts an Adam with an Eve in a perfect world, they blow it, ought to die, and he promises them a Savior. He lets a Joseph get tossed into a pit, sold as a slave, convicted for rape, and then appointed as the functional head of a world power. An entire nation—millions of people—go out at his behest into a desert, led for four decades by a cloud. He gives a donkey speech, holds the sun back for part of a day, and delivers food to a starving man via airmail. And then, he sends a special emissary—his own Son— who comes for the salvation of humanity, only to be murdered by the religious leaders of his day. The Babylonians, indeed.

Can a God like this be trusted? This is Habakkuk's question and ours. Marketplace pitfalls, ominous phone calls, the choices of teenagers, and the developments on X rays—because life is dangerous, sneaky, and notoriously unstable, we really need to know: Can God be trusted with life? And just what will that take?

A dynamic, nuanced faith that is robust enough to withstand storms, broad enough to accept Babylonians. Faith that gets you started with conversion and then stays with you through the process. For Habakkuk, that meant exposure to ideas about God that stretched conventional wisdom to the breaking point.

Is God cruel in this regard? Shouldn't God make life easy for his own? Why should he permit, much less cause, any sort of difficulty? These are hard questions and often raised. They deserve careful, thoughtful answers. Perhaps it is enough for now simply to draw a picture.

My daughter comes in from playing outside. She has been whirling about on our rickety wooden fort, built years ago by her grandfather and me. She is crying and pointing: It's her foot. The wood of that fort is dry and splintery, and in her foot is embedded an enormous chunk of timber. The wound is swollen and bleeding. "I can help," I say, and she begins to moan. "No," she pleads, "not that." She knows that I have removed splinters before, deep ones, and that the only way to do so is with a needle, or a clean knife. I pry or cut; it hurts. Not that, her eyes beg, but I cannot heed her. For the good of my daughter, I must excavate. She knows this, accepts it. I hold her leg and place a cube of ice near the entry point to dull the pain. Then I probe. The splinter is deep, and so I must go deep. She cries; I hold her foot securely. "Be still," I say, "even though this hurts. It is almost out," I assure her.

And then it is. A little blood comes from the tear in the skin, and I am holding between sticky red fingers a stub of wood. "Something this small brought that much pain?" I ask. She smiles a wet smile. We bandage the hole, and she runs back outside, healed, healthy. As the screen door slams, I rock back on my heels, reflecting that this is part of fathering: to press or even to cut so that greater good may come.

"I form the light and create darkness, I bring prosperity and create disaster; I, the LORD, do all these things" (Isa. 45:7). God is bigger than we know. We have to keep pulling back to see him, and just when we think we have captured all of him in the viewfinder, he expands. When our God is too small, the way he is fashioning good on our behalf or the sort of life he calls us to makes little sense. So pull back and look carefully. Notice the immediate strangeness of God's method, but notice also its coherence and effect. Building faith is serious business, a matter of life and death.

Faith demands the death of self, which the self, quite naturally, resists. This is why I need a big God and why he keeps sending me into the dark of howling storms and eerie quiet: I go there so that my faith will grow so that my self will die. At times, this process makes us feel like a top hurled out into the void to twirl, wobble, and clatter noisily, or collide with a hard surface. Here's a better image: Think of a yo-yo, flung far and spinning for sure, but connected.

A Better Perspective

Habakkuk shows his grasp of the situation by way of a subtle shift in his "second complaint." The prophet still has questions, but he begins by staring straight into the face of God and praying: O LORD (1:12). A prayer like this shows an understanding of linkage: The prophet looks up to God and starts with him; he is tethered and in submission to the Lord. There is little need then to forward an agenda or dominate the conversation with personal concerns. Habakkuk shows us a good way to start prayer, with the recognition that we walk, stand, sit, kneel, or lie before God, who is bigger than, more than, us. This shifts the focus and the question. It is no longer *why?* but *who?*

Who is this God on whom Habakkuk calls? Who is this one for whom even a gang as rowdy as the Babylonians can be pressed into constructive service? Who is this one whose association with such unsavory characters can result in desirable ends? What is there about this God that I don't understand but need to? Who is this strong and silent God?

When we can move from whining complaint to honest query, when we can break free from the gravity of our own concerns and push through to a broader view, insisting on noticing what God is up to, then we are making progress with faith. Too often we are self-consumed. Too often there is, to be brutally honest, no room for God's voice because our own is so loud.

Sometimes—perhaps often—our problem is one of perspective. We peer at a situation and do not see what is to our liking. So we raise a stink, attract a crowd. "Look!" we point out. "There is a problem here," we say to God. From our vantage point, we do see a problem, but the question is this: How accurate is our vantage point?

Look at clouds or river eddies or smoke: Do you see patterns? Occasionally. But typically they are little more than random swirls, right? Now probe this chaos with the tools of science and mathematics. We did not see patterns before because our sample was too small. But when we cast the net wide for all the data squirming like smelt and toss them into supercomputers for calculating and mapping, we begin to discern a beautiful, complex order. The resulting study of "chaos theory" starts to unfold, and pretty soon there are new university chairs given over to the study of previously "random" swirls. Weather reporting and aerodynamics, to name just two, will never be the same.

Sometimes our heads are so near the coffee table that we cannot make sense of the puzzle pieces. It's only when we pull back to take in the big picture that this little chink of blue or that little knob of brown fits. Earlier it was just another random piece of data; now it's part of a fence or the sky behind a chimney. Given the big picture, the right context, we can detect an obvious pattern.

For Habakkuk, the context is worship, and in this second exchange with God, he is reverent: "O Lord, are you not from everlasting?" (1:12). He has a wider screen up now and can see a God who is larger than any concern around him; he is a worshiper. There are still questions (1:13), but they are phrased in a new way. Now Habakkuk appears to be anticipating concerns others might raise, and he wants to be prepared as to how God might respond (2:1). Essentially these concerns revolve around the way God ought to deal with Babylon and the timetable for that. But note: Habakkuk's sense of urgency has dissipated; he is willing to stand at his watch and wait for what God has to say (2:1).

When the Lord replies, it is for the benefit of those Habakkuk has in mind; the prophet is given information that can be distributed to others (2:2). There are two points of interest here: First, the evildoers will be punished; second, the time for that is in the future. Beyond this, the Lord lays out his specific charges against Babylon, which makes clear the legitimacy of his intentions to destroy them.

God's "use" of Babylon is temporary; that nation will fall (this is the force of the "woes" starting at 2:9). When it comes time for "the earth . . . [to] be filled with the knowledge of the glory of the LORD" (2:14), there will be no room for the Babylonians to stand. The wage for sin is still death, sooner or later.

God has a timetable. He will not be rushed; neither will he be indifferent. "Though it linger, wait for it" (2:3), God counsels. Injustice concerns Habakkuk. God responds by taking him to a deeper level: Leave that to me, he seems to say. For you, settle this: Will you believe in God to the point that each day you give yourself over to that belief? Even when expectations are dashed, even when God's clear ways are ignored, will you place your faith in God? The arrogant do not, preferring their own strength, cleverness, or idols, but "the righteous will live by his faith" (2:4) [2] This is God's key point for Habakkuk and describes the life that pleases him.

The attempts we make to live without faith in God make sense in a way—the darkness is a frightening place to spend much time—but they are almost laughable. In the end, only God remains, the God who speaks to Habakkuk, to the disciples, to us. This One "is," existing perennially, and he is in his holy temple (2:20). Before him, all will eventually come and bow. So for now, quiet those desires that pull you away from what is good and true. Do not allow what is sense-able, whether it is your own abilities, a howling gale, a decadent culture, an erring child, a worrisome medical report, a meddlesome neighbor, an unreasonable boss, a fluctuating market, to sway you from your faith in God. Come before him, be silent (2:20), and live by faith.

It is an uncertain life, stretched by hardship and disrupted by quiet. Living by faith means walking in the dark, since faith is hardly necessary in the bright light of day, where all is clearly seen and known.

Think of it like this: When I manage a situation on my own, whether it is difficult or facile, I develop a measure of confidence for the next similar occurrence. So I can, for instance, rappel off a thirty-foot stone face in Argentina because I have in the past gone down ropes on the side of a gymnasium. My first time rappelling was terrifying as I stepped off the edge of that solid building; the next occasion was comparatively easy. When I come to the Argentinian cliff, I know what to expect: I've seen this before. I don't need faith, because I have experience.

But what if I suddenly learn that my job has been unexpectedly terminated—and I've never been fired, my kids are fast approaching college age, and I'm far from familiar networks? What if I'm standing in a little boat on a furious lake, about to be swamped by enormous waves? What if I look around, recognize cultural dissipation, call out for God, and get no response?

It was a walk in the dark for Habakkuk to believe God was still in control, particularly if this same God was about to employ Babylonians as his servants. This is why the Lord had to assure the prophet that the righteous live by faith. They keep going, God stresses, every day believing that God is real and that he matters. What they see around them should never be enough to persuade them otherwise.

A Life of Faith

In 1837, an English home welcomed a new baby boy. James Hudson Taylor would leave that home a scant eighteen years later, his heart indelibly marked by the Lord. By the age of twenty-one, Taylor was bound for China, where he would arrive after nearly six months of ocean travel. It was a land long closed to the gospel.

Taylor left a loving family, a promising career, and the comforts of British civilization to embark on a journey to a field few visited that would put him at odds with colleagues, strip his financial resources, bury his children, and break his health. Taylor would eventually die in China in 1905, a radiant man. Why?

Taylor's "spiritual secret"[3] was drawn from Habakkuk's experience: The righteous live by faith. For Taylor, having been apprehended by God's grace and made righteous, the only way life could possibly be lived was by faith in that same God. Otherwise it was without meaning and just too hard.

Taylor lived at a time when science and capitalism were flourishing. Charles Darwin's theories were entering the public arena, and Heinrich Schliemann was sparking new enquiry in archaeology. Alexander Graham Bell, Thomas Edison, and J. P. Morgan, pioneers of discovery and captains of industry, were carving new ways to look at life, new foci for centering life. Taylor might easily have applied his talents and energies to self-advancement or personal profit, but he chose a different route. He followed God, starting a mission that is now in its second century of existence. Thousands have served, thousands have converted, because of this faithfulness.

In faith, Hudson Taylor walked out on ice most others thought perilously thin. Along the way he was encouraged by people such as George Müeller, himself no mean representative of the life of faith, but he was also ridiculed and misunderstood. For Taylor, the life of faith meant abiding in God, counting on him to provide what was needed when it was needed. Difficulties were not ignored, but neither did they shape his life. That influence was reserved for God.

Faith in the Dark

By the end of this book, Habakkuk's faith has grown. We recognize this from the prophet's prayer, in which God is the focus (3:2–15). Habakkuk uses his estimable skills to craft a fine piece of powerful praise that, like all good art, connects with us even as it lifts us. It is both earthy and transcendent, and it serves as a benchmark for prayers.

We do not often pray like Habakkuk. A friend spoke once of a church near him: "Three services Sunday morning, but they could have the weekly prayer meeting in my car." I couldn't disagree; my experience with church-sponsored prayer meetings was similar. Why? The answer lies no farther away than my own heart. My wife asks me to meet her for prayer, about our family, our future. Sure, I say. Later, when there is less to do.

Small faith—the idea that God is not quite as important or necessary as other aspects of my life—keeps me from prayer. God wants to disrupt this self-centeredness, wants to ripple faith through my life like fudge through vanilla ice cream—faith that counts him as real, powerful, lovely, interested, worth my time and energy. When I hold in faith to a God like that, I will worship, and I will pray.

Faith and worship are symbiotic. The God we cry out for, the God we need in crisis, the God we want in order to make sense of even the mundane—he is the God we draw near and stay near in faith. We might be tempted to trust our own devices, or be lulled into complacency, or be crusted by rebellion, but deep down, when we're quiet, we want sufficient mass at the center of our life to attract and hold us. It sounds like a black hole, toward which faith pushes and pulls us. This is a good picture, because as we yield to the force of faith, we do get drawn in. Against our will? No. We gladly approach the one who draws. In faith, we come nearer, slipping over the edge. Into . . . what?

The dark. Faith always means darkness for our life, but not perpetual darkness. This is where the black hole image no longer serves. There are still troubles, still bad days at the office, still flat tires and whiny kids and homework; there are dark times that challenge us. But we comprehend the darkness; we understand its purpose. We need not fear the dark, for God is near. We may not always detect his presence, and he may not speak as often as we'd like, but we are not abandoned.

Between Portillo, Chile, and Mendoza, Argentina, blacktop paves a mountain pass and descends to follow the contours of the Andes. From this road one can see the *Cordillera* mountain range in all its splendor. Along the way, tunnels core the mountain sides. As one drives, dazzled by the sun reflecting off snowcaps, one suddenly enters such a tunnel. It's a remote area in an impoverished land; there are no electric lights, and you are suddenly blind. This road to Mendoza reminds me of the journey of faith: Bright light sometimes; utter darkness sometimes; the sun shining always, whether I see it or not.

Habakkuk—the name means something like "embrace" in English—had pressed his life into service of God. He knows the dark times, when "the fig tree does not bud and there are no grapes on the vines, . . . the olive crop fails and the fields produce no food, . . . there are no sheep in the pen and no cattle in the stalls," but this is not enough to rock his world off its hinges.

"I will rejoice in the LORD, I will be joyful in God my Savior" (3:17–18), he affirms, embracing the God who builds his faith.

Furious storms challenge faith, so do the subtlety of stillness and the strangeness of an unexpected word. The life of faith is lived under frequently changing skies. Like Habakkuk, like the disciples, we can by faith continue to live, moving through the dark, calling out, listening, waiting. We may not fully understand what is going on or why, but we can trust the *who:* God is the one who cares, the one who builds, the one who enables us to stand on firm ground in high places (3:19).

$$\overline{3}$$

ABANDON PRIDE
Obadiah

One of faith's greatest enemies is pride. Pride is like pollution: There is widespread recognition of its effect but great reluctance to do away with the cause. Epidemic, pride pervades our individual psyche and corporate culture. As proof, check the neighborhood sidewalk. There, along with the random collection of paw prints and bicycle tracks, you will find an intentional display of names. New cement, like the sides of barns, broad tree trunks, or exposed rock faces towering above sea level, begs decoration, and the most frequent adornment is a name. Names are scratched there by people announcing themselves to all who pass by: I was here. Don't forget me.

The problem of pride is also insidious. It wafts from the arrogant and the preeners, polluting us and sullying our environment. "Don't get cocky, kid," Han Solo warns Luke Skywalker, but it is too late: The barn door's open and that horse has run.

Pride might become socially acceptable when buried beneath false humility or masked by "philanthropy." But it's like a hamster, forever seeking ways to escape. Give it a chance and pride will break out of the cage we halfheartedly build.

We don't carve grocery lists on trees, or etch mathematical formulae into wet cement, or paint assembly instructions for jungle gyms on the sides of barns. We leave our name. There is room for, or thought of, little else. Pride is the urge to stand alone, to stand above all else. It inevitably crowds other people into an increasingly small space; it blinds one to the value of God. Pride is the natural enemy of faith.

The Consequence of Pride

"1 abhor the pride of Jacob" (Amos 6:8). This is God speaking, expressing distaste for the way this community of faith has so easily cast off its moral values and social responsibilities. Having abandoned the care of the needy to pursue instead the comfort of self, the children of Israel—the descendants of Jacob—have supplanted faith with pride.

The same is true for Jacob's brother, Esau. So God hands a message to Obadiah, announcing that the pride of Edom has preceded his fall:

> "The pride of your heart has deceived you,
>   you who live in the clefts of the rocks
>   and make your home on the heights,
> you who say to yourself,
>   'Who can bring me down to the ground?'
> Though you soar like the eagle
>   and make your nest among the stars,
>   from there I will bring you down," declares the LORD.
>
> OBADIAH 3–4

Here is the book's first irony: A message we need is easily ignored. Of the Bible's five one-chapter books—a letter from Paul and Timothy to Philemon, two epistles of John, Jude, and Obadiah—

the last surely ranks as the most obscure of the bunch. Who can get all that interested in a brief vision about the fate of Edom at the hands of God? Okay, so Edom is another name for Esau, Jacob's twin, hirsute brother. But after that, what can we say? Why trouble with Edom, even for only a single chapter?

It helps to go back to the earlier, slightly more familiar stories about Jacob and Esau. We meet these two, shortly before their birth, through prophecies about them: "One people will be stronger than the other, and the older will serve the younger" (Gen. 25:23). It is a recipe for disaster, this promise of strength, that prediction of ranking—these guys entered the world with trouble brewing. It soon boiled over. Jacob tricked his older, stronger brother, Esau, out of a lucrative financial settlement and then had to run away. Years later they made amends, but Jacob kept a wary eye on his brother and plenty of distance between them.

In subsequent generations, this animosity simmered and occasionally flared, like the time Jacob's descendants, newly released from four hundred years of captivity in Egypt, asked permission to cross Esau's borders in order to shorten their trip to the Promised Land. "You may not pass through here," they were told. "If you try, we will march out and attack you" (Num. 20:18). Edom sounded a little touchy; maybe they remembered past injustices, or perhaps they had heard a few bars from Miriam's song, "The chiefs of Edom will be terrified" (Exod. 15:15), as God's holy people marched through neighboring territory.

By Obadiah's time[1] the rift was total. Edom had no love for Israel; no brotherly affection remained. I think of a touching commercial that advertised candy bars. Two brothers strolling the deck of a large cruise ship share a treat, and as the music swells, one takes the hand of the other—they are friends, linked by blood and chocolate. But if this were Jacob and Esau, one would have pushed the other overboard.

"A friend loves at all times, and a brother is born for adversity" (Prov. 17:17). This aphorism explains God's intentions: When difficulties arise, friends should be consistent, family should be available. The breakdown of such relationships spells disaster for all concerned. In our day, family dysfunction is more readily excused, though no less detrimental, and a proverb such as this sounds curiously quaint. But for God, such trouble is troubling. It causes pain. It is caused, most often, by pride.

God sends Obadiah with a message about Edom's fate. He will not condone pride that snaps limbs from the family tree, nor will he stand idly by when that pride threatens to eclipse him. As Jesus made plain, the people of God are meant for a life lived low. "Come follow me," Jesus says, and recognize from the outset that there is, properly, someone ahead of—and above—you.

Place Service ahead of Pride

Naaman demonstrated the trenchant nature of pride when he found himself at the end of his own capacity to fix a problem (the full story is in 2 Kings 5). Naaman's problem was leprosy, and he had come to Israel—at the suggestion of an unnamed servant girl—to seek help from the prophet Elisha. The prophet had instructed this military commander to wash himself in the Jordan River, an act the man deemed more onerous than trampling a troubling city. He whines, "Are not Abana and Pharpar, the rivers of Damascus, better than any of the waters of Israel? Couldn't I wash in them and be cleansed?" (2 Kings 5:12).

It is only by adhering to the prophet's counsel that the soldier can be cured. Only when he lowers himself, literally and figuratively, will he see the pain of his life melt away. Naaman thought to handle things his way. Hadn't he been successful in so many campaigns already? But this trouble is persistent and departs only one way.

Will Naaman avail himself of the cure? Or will he insist on something more suited to his station? The reader does not have long to wait, for the companions of Naaman (the text calls them "servants") offer advice, which the man deigns to take. He dips in the Jordan, seven times so that the point will be driven home, and emerges with baby-smooth skin.

What should we take from this story? That God likes to confound the wise? That distasteful tasks await those who seek better things? Or that we are all sick to the point of oozing filth, and that no amount of lotion or washing or clothing will hide this, that no measure of personal industry or cleverness will fix this, that the only way we can ever hope to get better is if we get off our high horse and bend low in the river?

Naaman shows that the cure for the dread disease of pride is not pretty. It requires submersion, submission. Jesus pointed to this in his teaching, saying things such as "the Son of Man did not come to be served, but to serve" (Mark 10:45). We gloss over this, forgetting how radical a concept it was. Naaman was more honest: I'm not going there!

"There" is not simply a muddy river. It is a life of profound anonymity, where pride's insistence on self must fade. This is the only cure for the superating self: service, where we bend pride to the breaking point, snapping its hold over us. It is no easy task. Our innate desire is to vault service and vaunt self; we make deals too, promising to serve now so long as we rise later.

Edom stood tall and proud. This nation thought their superior might made them apt lords, but the Lord said no. "You should not look down on your brother; you should not boast so much; you should not march like victors, or seize the wealth of others" (Obadiah 12–13, paraphrase mine). God wants people who will serve others, esteem them. He is after those who will stand *for* the small, not over them. When that posture is forgotten or abused, God is not pleased, and judgment follows. The goal for successful living is not mastery or even success, but service.

Jesus indicates the primary place of service with his teaching:

> Suppose one of you had a servant plowing or looking after the sheep. Would he say to the servant when he comes in from the field, "Come along now and sit down to eat"? Would he not rather say, "Prepare my supper, get yourself ready and wait on me while I eat and drink; after that you may eat and drink"? Would he thank the servant because he did what he was told to do? So you also, when you have done everything you were told to do, should say, "We are unworthy servants; we have only done our duty."
>
> Luke 17:7–10

Servants relinquish their rights. Their positions are dependent entirely on their master. Their lives are lived according to the master's direction. These are difficult concepts for people raised in a free society and who have imbued the principles and counted on the privileges of a democracy. That is why Jesus must be so strict: He must break through not only cultural hesitations but also innate yearnings that have been deformed by sin. The result of sin is that the service we should have rendered from the submission we should have offered is eclipsed by pride. This is why Jesus brings out the big guns: He seeks to kill, and not merely wound, pride.

As we wrestle with his teaching, we must also face squarely the example of his life. This Paul explicates in Philippians 2, where Jesus, "precisely because he was in the form of God, did not consider being equal with God grounds for grasping. On the contrary, he rather poured himself out by taking the form of a slave."? This description follows the reminder that our attitude is to be the same as that of Christ (Phil. 2:5). We who are his followers are also to carry in our hearts the willingness to serve, to the point of pouring ourselves honestly and completely into the person and work of the servant.

This is difficult to swallow. Few of us would report an inherent desire to bend toward another's will; few of us willingly take up the basin and towel of the slave. A life of servitude is not what most envision for their careers, and given the choice, we'd prefer to be Bruce Wayne over Alfred any day of the week. We who are so eager to "follow Jesus" still balk at the most fundamental level. We will stay in his wake as long as it means a good ride here and a good time there, but we grow discontented when the Master steers us to a different place.

We need to get over ourselves, or, perhaps better, to come under him. "Accepting Jesus" is not simply a matter of saying yes to a really good bargain. It is a matter of having him bring out the long knives that cut our selves down to size. In pride, we are too big for God; humility recognizes the need we have that pride routinely attempts to mask.

Once we submit to God, by recognizing our need for him (it's not just a good idea—we *need* God), then we can get about the business of living. It will not be life as usual, because that sort of life is, by definition, powered by pride. Instead, it will be a life of faith in which we trust God more than self. It will be a life lived low in which we take the form of a servant.

This is a problem, but only for pride.

To Be Great, Be a Servant

In the first class of my freshman year at college, a professor walked in and immediately took a poll. How many of you were your high school's valedictorian? Several hands shot up. Salutatorian? More hands. Class president? Hands. Yearbook editor? Hands. Two-, three-, or four-letter athletes? Hands. Youth group leaders? Hands. And frowns. Initially, we liked this exercise: It helped us help others determine our worth in terms of our accomplishments. The categories our professor mentioned had been convenient ways of establishing our place within our own contexts—and many of us had risen above most others. We knew that, noticed it, liked it. But by the end of this exercise, we sullenly realized that we who had been big fish in home ponds were now in a much larger sea and swimming next to fish who looked a lot like us. What would set us apart—or more accurately, above—those in the new space we now occupied?

This was our professor's point, which, come to find out, was not far from the heart of Jesus. Two disciples came to him one day, asking for the honor of proximity. How dare they, the other ten fumed. They probably meant, Why didn't *I* think of that?

Jesus blew their concerns—the concerns of them all—into the dust. "Whoever wants to become great among you must be your servant, and whoever wants to be first must be your slave" (Matt. 20:26–27). Words such as these deflate people full of hot air—people like you and me who think we ought to have better, who believe we warrant the best.

I was sitting in my office one day. After years of working in the basement at my house, I had finally moved over to the building our church had recently been given. It was a step up, I thought, into a space of my own. Except that I would share this space with a Sunday morning class of kids who left their art on the walls, their crumbs on the floor, and their fingerprints on the desk. *My* walls, *my* floor, *my* desk, that is.

So I sat there in my chair—the swiveling office chair that was *mine,* but that had been readjusted by some kid from the previous day's class—and my mind got going. Look at this place, I thought, eyes passing over the glitter trapped in faded carpet and lighting on the mismatched furniture. I'm the pastor here; I helped this organization get off the ground. Surely I deserve better than secondhand goods in shared space. At which point a strong voice pierced my heart. What you deserve, this voice impressed, is death. Suddenly life became a lot clearer.

Here I sat in my smugness, arrogant enough to pass judgment on kids, church members, brothers, and sisters. I was willing to put them in their place so that I could have mine. What I forgot was where my place was: near the ground, at the feet, on the cross.

Pride keeps me insecure regarding my place with God. It tries to rise up and create something that he will appreciate, that he—and others, truth be told—cannot help but notice. Servants, instead, gladly go about their business, content in the knowledge of what they are about. Their reputation is of little account; what matters is their relationship to the master. Servants need not think themselves of no account; rather, they are to consider carefully the full impact of submission. When they submit to another—when they give place to a Master other than themselves—they can still go on living. It is just that now they do not live for themselves.

Self Must Give Way to God

The French mystic Simone Weil spoke of submission as "decreation," a process by which we unravel the twine with which pride has entangled our selves. Weil suggests that "once we have understood we are nothing, the object of all our efforts is to become nothing." How different this is from "conventional wisdom." How liberating. Weil even claims that in the decreating, we make way for something lively: "We have to die in order to liberate a tied up energy."[3]

This draws us back to Obadiah's touchstone: Self must give way to God. When that understanding gets muddled or when self dominates, sin is not far behind. Because God cares too much to let sin go unchecked, he sends prophets to signal the need for change. They are the lighthouses warning tankers that unless they alter course, they are destined to run aground. With Weil we see that the course correction is severe—all the way to death. From Obadiah, we learn that it is merely the death of self-centered pride.

This is tough, because we'd rather not see ourselves in these terms. We are more comfortable being Jesus' friends, confidants, or emissaries; we'd prefer not to deal with all this servant language. But that cannot be avoided. As quick as we are to be in the inner circle, we must be equally at home on the outer ring where we serve at table without any immediate reward. Is there a way to fit the two together?

Only one. If we are to come to the place where Jesus can call us friend, "it is necessary to uproot oneself. To cut down the tree and make of it a cross, and then to carry it every day."[4] This happens in the valley of death, where we slay the self that is so opposed to serving. It is a frightening place, full of shadow, because light cannot break in until the self inducing an eclipse diminishes. But even here, in the valley of death's shadows, God is near. He is ready to help those ready to serve.[5]

Why would Jesus speak so resolutely about servants, cutting them no slack? Because he wants his followers to be so willing to follow him that they gladly forego their own selves. This has the sound of a military strategy—of boot camp, where the new recruit is badgered into submission for the eventual good of his unit. There is no place in this force for private thoughts, for independent action. What makes you effective, what saves your group, is unswerving attention to the commander. He speaks; you jump.

We get to thinking that service is the state one comes to after years of maturing with the Lord. Not so. Service is the lesson the new recruit fresh off the bus is meant to learn. Get it straight, and right now. Remember, Edom is being judged for a failure to serve—Edom, who grew alongside Jacob, in Isaac's house, where God was Lord. Esau should have learned the lesson, should have known that God valued service over self. He didn't. He paid.

No wonder the call to servanthood needs to be so loud. It gets drowned out by the swell of our own names because we would much rather make our own mark than help someone else leave theirs. Serve? No thanks. I'd rather sit. Oh, and can you bring me a soda?

Which brings us back to Obadiah and a second irony: The message on pride in this little book is delivered by one who is obscure. About all we know of the messenger is his name, and it may actually be that we do not even know that. *Obadiah* is Hebrew for the English phrase "servant of God" and may function as a pseudonym of one who is quietly saying, I am God's humble servant. Like Peter Wimsey's man Bunter,[6] he is present when needed but content to stay in the background, indistinct.

No One Is Obscure

The production of a motion picture means the hiring of screenwriters, the scouting for scenery, contracts with stars, and lining up caterers. It also requires extras, people who fill space. They have no lines; their names don't roll in the credits, and sometimes even what they do never appears in the film. My daughter had a teacher who was hired as an extra for a television show being made nearby. He relayed to the class how he had gone downtown, waited around, finally had his scene shot, and went home. He told the class when to expect the episode. We joined our daughter at the appointed time and watched the TV intently for the entire hour. No sign of this man. The next day our daughter came back with the news that his scene had been cut.

Might a servant be similarly unnecessary and expendable? We think so and fear it. We fear life as an "extra," preferring instead a leading role or at least a speaking part. We could not bear ending up on the cutting room floor either, and so we do all we can to be noticed, distinct.

Obscurity is a secret fear for many, and one more enemy of pride. If I successfully bury myself in God, will I give up all my uniqueness as a person? It can feel as though this is the result, and because of that, many balk. But there is another way. Consider instead that slaying pride means I no longer have to vaunt myself, no longer have to jockey for position. I can, as a servant of God, gladly take the place he assigns to carry out the tasks he prepares. While some of these—perhaps many—may appear to be mundane or nonglamorous, that assessment really says more about my value system than his. What is more important, an atom or a sun? Which is the most valuable pixel on a monitor screen? Is a finger worth more than a spleen?

"If anyone speaks, he should do it as one speaking the very words of God. If anyone serves, he should do it with the strength God provides, *so that in all things* God may be praised" (1 Peter 4:11, emphasis added). An emphasis on service changes the equation from considering value to examining role. I acknowledge the rightful director, producer, and casting agent of this film and cheerfully take the place assigned. I recognize that in God's scripting, no person is ever considered an extra, since each particular individual has inestimable value. This is the lesson Obadiah had learned: He apparently was content to be a mouthpiece for God and have no other aspect of his surely wonderful self emerge.

We rail against this, of course—even in the church. In fact, it is in the church that pride has reared its head so often. Think back to high school and Geoffrey Chaucer's *Canterbury Tales,* in which the poet ridiculed the indulgences of clergy such as the Friar:

> For in so eminent a man as he
> It was not fitting with the dignity
> Of his position, dealing with a scum
> Of wretched lepers; nothing good can come
> Of commerce with such slum-and-gutter dwellers,
> But only with the rich and victual-sellers.
> But anywhere a profit might accrue
> Courteous he was and lowly of service, too.[7]

Chaucer's charge cuts across denominational lines and is as current as the latest religious scandal. The look of pride may vary from group to group, but its smell lingers. Christians have grappled with this for centuries, and groups of heretics have left the Christian church when their commitment to pride grew too strong. The

Gnostics, who planted seeds as the New Testament autographs circulated during the post-apostolic age, are one such example.

Gnostics claimed special knowledge about spiritual matters, such as the way a transcendent, holy God could effectively communicate with material beings. With elaborate ritual and through laborious reasoning, Gnostics indoctrinated newcomers so that they too could be "in the know." But carve away the trappings of a quasi-religious experience and it's still a shell game: We know something you don't. And that's pride talking.

The Gnostics and their ilk don't bother us enough. We still long to be on the inside, different, better. Pride still blinds us to the incredible privilege of being included in God's family; it still wants us to be dissatisfied until we are dominant. The cement shows us this, with those names laboriously etched against the fear of fading to the vanishing point.

A New and Better Name

Obadiah was content to let his name slip away into obscurity. Or to be more accurate, to allow his name to be absorbed in one that was even better, for when Obadiah calls attention to the sovereign Lord, he is saying, this is my Master, and who I am is tied up in who he is.

When people respond to God's call and join his family, they are reborn. Then, as with any new thing, they receive a name. It's a new name. They were given one name at their physical birth, and they receive another when they are born in the spiritual sense. This is what Isaiah means (62:2) and what Jesus says to John (Rev. 2:17). Such adherents are not simply "people of the Book," and so on common ground with those of other "world faiths." It goes deeper. They are people of the name, of God, who gave his name to them. Those who come to him are no longer known only by their own names but by his.

This new name conveys an important message. When one joins the family of God, identity—worth, even—is derived. It is not self-generated but accorded because of proximity to God. Now, that's not such a bad deal. Fortunes have been made, careers launched, and futures secured on the basis of a good patronymic. But it does have its implications.

Consider the "household of Aristobulus" mentioned in Romans 16:10.[8] We do not hear the names of individuals in this group, but we do know that they are connected with one Paul esteems. What is true of Aristobulus is true of those who are with him at his home. So it is with the people of God. We are "members of God's household" (Eph. 2:19) and as such are connected with him. It does not matter that our individual characteristics are not bathed in limelight. What matters is our connection with God, as we serve in and through this household.

Our name, then, is folded into God's own. We become like people at the company picnic, decked out in T-shirts and caps bearing the firm's logo. Our own names are not as important as our association.

Satisfaction in Serving

We must draw this into our heart as an antidote to pride: the desire to serve that is satisfied by serving. We cannot even bow to serving for a time or purpose, thinking it a temporary role that will inevitably result in a "better" position. Rather, we accept what God hands out and leave all else in his hands.

Like Joseph. Born to a family of dominant males, Joseph ends up in a pit, from which point he is sold as a slave as a concession to those who prefer to kill him. Joseph lands on his feet in Egypt, in the home of Potiphar, an important Egyptian official. Slavery in Potiphar's house isn't home, but then home wasn't all that great. So Joseph goes along, until Potiphar's wife makes a play for the young man. Joseph refuses, and she, spurned, lashes out. As a result, he spends the next several years in jail.

What ran through Joseph's mind day after interminable day? The Scripture says little about his thinking but much about his action: Joseph served (check the story in Genesis 39–40). He served Potiphar's house, and then he served the warden, and then upon his eventual release he served all of Egypt. Did the events he faced fit Joseph's own plan for advancement? Of course not. He served because he must have come, along the way, to terms with the reality that a life of service was exactly what God wanted of him.

We must come to the place where we say, "I will serve." When we do that, we put pride on notice. Should God choose to elevate us, that's his business. Our serving does not obligate him to do so, although the biblical witness would suggest that God tends to find his leaders among those truly willing to humble themselves. But still we cannot lose sight of the obscure: There are plenty of people who served without any advancement in social standing.

Think of the New Testament Joseph, who was asked to serve as a father for Jesus. What do we know of him? Very little, other than that he was willing to do what was asked of him without protest. Martha was a servant too, though she raised a small protest on occasion. Barnabas, who according to early records was a man of considerable standing, gets the job of mentoring Paul, which means that he shrinks farther and farther into the distance. And Paul himself, despite his obvious strengths and accomplishments, thought of himself most often in these terms.

Church history is packed with people committed to serve. Some of their stories are known, but many more never appear in print or on video. Occasionally one meets such people—veterinarians in Ethiopia who walk away from the prospect of a lucrative practice to teach basic health to preliterates, school teachers in Ecuador who plunge deeper into the bush to learn a difficult language, single moms who forge homes where God is honored, retirees who forego golf to pastor small churches—the people of God, called to serve, doing so with distinction to the point of becoming indistinct.

Make Room for God

Here is the crowning irony: In the end, the almighty God of the universe comes only to those who have room for him. Once pride falls to humility, we are finally in a place where God can work with us, welcome us, share himself with us. I cannot be a friend of God as long as I am a friend only to myself, and as long as I am self-consumed, I will miss so much of what he has and wants for me.

In the mid-eighties, the Lord led me to help a small group start a church. We moved to a new state, linked with an existing church, and began the legwork. Shortly after we identified our "target location," I read a newspaper account of a fellow who, after extensive research into planting a church somewhere in the nation, had, with the help of his home church in California, traveled to our state, to our town, to begin. He was six months ahead of my schedule and better funded.

I called to set up lunch; I went with a slight swagger, prepared to position myself, ready to compete. The man I met disarmed me with his gentle humility. Over time, he proved his intentions, persisted in being friendly, generous, and encouraging. When I needed photocopies, he offered his machine. When my computer went down, his was available. A car? A meeting place? A listening ear? All gladly given by one willing to serve. He didn't keep score; he sought no recognition.[9] Over time, his incarnation of Jesus' servant heart helped to soften me, bled off the pride that bubbled up in me so often, opened space in me the Lord could fill. I finally realized the futility of pride's insistence that we be competitors. We were, instead, colleagues, called to serve the same Master. That lunch became a monthly meeting for ten years; today, we are fast friends.

Release pride? That changes everything. Now the energy consumed by putting up a brave front can be channeled elsewhere, such as into welcoming God, or serving people who have pressing needs. Pride ignores this mutuality. Esau should have been looking out for his little brother; instead, he picked on him. When Esau's people found his brothers an easy mark, the aggravation intensified: He held him in disdain, robbed his meager wealth, harried his feeble constituents (Obadiah 13–14). Brotherly kindness fell victim to pride.

The Lord seeks people—like my friend, like Naaman—who will abandon pride. He raises people who will call for this way of life. Obadiah was one, the apostle Paul another. "As a prisoner of the Lord, then, I urge you to live a life worthy of the calling you have received," says Paul. It is a life in which you are "completely humble and gentle" (Eph. 4:1–2). God uses people like this, servants who can doff pride and don humility. He befriends them too.

"I no longer call you servants, but friends" (John 15:15). "No longer"? Once Jesus' disciples learned these lessons, they came to be viewed differently by him. It wasn't that they finally passed the course in service and could graduate to something else; rather, they had grown accustomed to life as servants and therefore were sufficiently trustworthy as to be counted friends.

Esau refused to learn this, so in the end, he relinquished his position and was driven away. "The kingdom will be the LORD's" (Obadiah 21), and in this kingdom only servants who are finished with pride can stand.

4

USE POWER WELL
Micah

*I*t should be possible to direct with humility, to be a true servant-leader. Demanding, tricky, rare, even, but possible. This is Micah's contention, and the reason he comes barreling into high courts and common streets with his searing indictments (1:3–5). The kings of his time should have done better, but both north and south suffered from leaders who ran after pagan gods, forged expedient political treaties, or enlarged their own holdings. Those attitudes trickled down to their subordinates, who in turn made life miserable for those in their care.

Power, even political power, comes from God (Prov. 21:1; John 19:11) and is to be used for good. This is why Micah blasts the abusers: "Woe to those who plan iniquity, to those who plot evil on their beds! At morning's light they carry it out because it is in their power to do it. They covet fields and seize them, and houses, and take them" (Micah 2:1–2). Under them, the led watch their holdings diminish and their lives erode. Micah cannot stand for this. "Should you not know justice, you who hate good and love evil; who tear the skin from my people and the flesh from their bones?" he demands (3:1–2).

It's a double-edged question. On the one hand, Micah challenges leaders to endorse the standard of justice with which they have been entrusted. On the other, he promises that they will be subjected to judgment, precisely because of their failure to use their power well (see 3:9–12).

Micah envisions a time when all will live under God's hand, basking in the glory of power rightly used (chap. 4). This will be ushered in by a benevolent ruler "whose origins are from of old" (5:2).[1] This one will "shepherd his flock in the strength of the LORD. . . . And he will be their peace" (5:4–5). He will serve as the paradigm for how God acts and what God wants.

Remember What God Has Done

An insurance salesman had the seat next to mine in a jostling tour van. We were part of a small group that had been inspecting a Costa Rican volcano, and now we were heading back to town. He and I asked about respective vocations, and then talk turned to God. My companion had been around the religion block; he had read, thought, dialogued, and decided to bow out, content with being a cheerful skeptic. For him, the problem with God turned on a view of his involvement with humanity. He doesn't really get involved, this salesman suggested, because if he did, that would prove he had made a mistake earlier. Miracles, said my companion, are just examples of God having to undo an unforeseen development.

I begged to differ, and the two of us chatted amiably until the ride ended. He wished me well in my efforts to communicate with people like him; I encouraged him to continue his search for God, because the God he needs to find and know is one who does good (Micah 6:8). He intervenes, not because he made a mistake that requires repair but because he cares about the people involved.

Many people have peculiar ideas about God. Apparently, Micah's audience thought of him as a cosmic bully who simply wanted to whomp on them and make their lives miserable. That elicits a howl from God: "My people, what have I done to you? How have I burdened you? Answer me" (6:3).

Far from oppressing them, God had worked consistently for their good. By way of illustration, he takes them back to Egypt, where they had been trapped by the gravity of that world power's enormous mass. On their own, God's children could not escape the pull of tyrants determined to keep them under control. In anguish they cried out (Exod. 2:23; 3:7, 9), and then God stepped in with powerful signs and wonders that snapped the oppressors' locks and opened the door to freedom. Moses explained the reasons for and implications of the rescue:

> It was because the LORD loved you and kept the oath he swore to your forefathers that he brought you out with a mighty hand and redeemed you from the land of slavery. . . . Those who hate him he will repay to their face by destruction. . . . Therefore, take care to follow the commands, decrees and laws I give you today.
>
> DEUTERONOMY 7:8, 10–11

Egypt. Can you go back into the mud pits of your ancestors and feel their backs bend and break under the strain of forced labor? Can you sense their despair as their homeland is taken from them and turned into a gulag? Can you taste the gnawing in the stomach, brought on by too many sparse meals? Can you hear the mothers wailing over the death of their infant sons?

Micah says, "Remember" (6:4–8). And then, recall what God did. He sent Moses, the lad drawn from water and set like a cool drink into Pharoah's palace. Raised to be king, he turned instead to champion the oppressed. He was banished for this, and so a man twice exiled. But in the barrenness of Midian's desert, Moses met God. There in the land that spawned the traders who brought Joseph to Egypt in the first place, Moses met the one who would bring about release from slavery. Miracles piled on top of miracles, until finally greedy Pharoah let them go.

Moses, Aaron, Miriam—three heroes who stood against the madness of Pharoah and brought in God's own Word. Who led the throng of whiners, who put up with people unaccustomed to success, to freedom. Who watched the pillars of cloud and fire, who supervised the caravan, who settled disputes. Remember! Taste the water flowing from a rock, bread fresh from heaven, meat plucked from the air. Shudder at the shrieks as snakes strike the recalcitrant. Do you see the serpent lifted high on a pole? This is your God—terrible, powerful, demanding; gracious, generous, strong. He releases. He redeems.

And you choose idols? You have lost sight of God and his kindness, and as a result, you have yourselves grown hard and harsh. You have loomed over others—your own brothers and sisters—to demand from them what once you could not pay yourselves. This only shows how depraved you are. Having lost sight of God, you have eyes only for yourselves.

He has shown you what is good. Those poles for Asherah that impale the ground, those high places preserved for an endless array of Baals—can they ever hope to show you anything? Are they capable of producing good? God alone has shown you what is good.

What radiates from God is an abundance of good—the standard for good. By comparison, what we manufacture to be good pales; what we often seek, thinking it good, has no moment. There is no denying that we are occupied by interest in the "good": Our philosophers and poets have consistently pointed us to it and revealed our fascination with it. But to appreciate good, we must look at God.

He has shown you. The tense implies past action that has a lingering effect. What he showed you in Egypt still has significance for today, says Micah, because it emphasizes the wonder-working nature of God, trumpets his commitment to redemption. It is told so often, perhaps, because people are like young cooks in the kitchen. In their eagerness to whip up something unique, personal—new!—they forget the basic ingredients.

Act Justly

He has shown you what is good. Now, what does God require of you? Something, we are certain of that. We have lived long enough to know that there is no free lunch; the piper must be paid.

Let's see: How about some burnt offerings or yearlings? Perhaps I could demonstrate the depth of my contrition—or the breadth of my holdings—by herding thousands of rams before the priests or carting in wagon loads of oil. And then, if I were truly penitent, truly devout, truly interested in making a really good impression, I might even offer—my child. No greater sacrifice would be possible!

Efforts such as these (6:6–7) make no impact on the Lord. It is neither a matter of quality nor quantity: God is after a personal commitment to imitation rather than a public display of affection. What does the Lord require? When the question was asked of Jesus, he replied, "Do not commit adultery, do not murder, do not steal, do not give false testimony. Honor your parents." Then came the retort: "All this I have done from my youth!" Jesus probes further, prying open this young man's heart: "One thing you lack. Go, sell everything you have and give to the poor" (Mark 10:21).[2]

Jesus turned away a bright prospect for the kingdom because the young man refused to part with his wealth. It wasn't that Jesus was opposed to having wealthy people in his kingdom; he freely received financial support from many who were well off.[3] What the Lord wanted from this "rich ruler" (one version of his story appears in Luke 18:18–30) was a release of money's grip. What does the Lord require of you? Whatever has hold of your heart other than him. God knows that when he has your heart, good—like justice and mercy—can flow from your life.

In Egypt, Pharoah abused his power. He could have been a force for good, shaping the extraordinary resources presented by an expatriate nation residing in his land. Instead, he chose to subject people to harsh labor and to remove their freedoms and pleasures. Power is meant to be exercised for the benefit of others. Pharoah used it to forward his own agenda.

Justice demands that people are accorded the value they deserve. Justice acts to right wrongs visited upon one person or group by another. To act justly means to use the available power, influence, and resources in such a way that those for whom you have responsibility benefit. The perversion of justice comes when you suck dry the wells of such people in order to irrigate your own gardens.

That's what Micah noticed and could not abide. Those whose ancestors had felt the lash in Egypt because of an unjust exercise of power had themselves, in the prophet's day, become the oppressors. Given opportunity to mete justice for the needy, they chose instead to become malevolent lords. They had forgotten the basics; they had lost sight of Egypt's lessons; they had stopped noticing God's goodness.

Shame on them, we think. We, who can easily cut another down to size when it pleases us. We, who rarely think about the impact our words, our sneers, our casual glances of disdain can have. We, who snag a bargain at the expense of a mistreated laborer, who lay inordinate demands on our subordinates, who overlook the "service staff," who wrap ourselves in cashmere afghans and sink into leather easy chairs while many nearby shiver outside. Shame on them?

In high school I held a position of influence for a time. I can't remember exactly why, but what I do recall is the way I once used this power. A new kid had moved with his family to our country. Like the rest of us "expatriates," he was far from home and the familiar. To complicate matters, he had some distinguishing characteristics that were easy to mimic and to mock. This we did, my clique and I, until he was beside himself with frustration. We congratulated ourselves on our cleverness, indifferent to what was going on in him—until one morning, when I stood talking with my compatriots. Out of the corner of my eye I caught a blur. It was this guy, streaking toward me, full throttle, intent on demonstrating his irritation. He dropped to the ground and skidded, in a perfect sliding tackle, catching my leg in the tangle of his. I went down. There was a hush as I lay there, dazed. I rose to my feet and stumbled; I could barely walk. My knee reminds me still of my failure to act justly with this person.

Power is not a tool to be manipulated but a gift to be shared. I am to use whatever power I am accorded for the benefit of others. A few politicians understand this *noblesse oblige,* a few artisans, a few financiers. Too many are wrapped in the trappings of power, attempting to make it grow like interest in a bank and to use it for personal gain. "Let [leaders] govern diligently," Paul counsels in Romans 12:8. A better translation uses the adjective "generously," or "liberally," because leaders are meant to use their means to broadcast goodness. When we come to power on these terms, we will be very close to justice.

William Wilberforce understood this. Born to wealth and privilege, he could have remained an anonymous figure in an obscure British Parliament. God had other plans. He broke into Wilberforce's life, saving him under the ministry of John Wesley[4] and surrounding him with people such as William Pitt and John Newton, who stirred his passions and channeled his energy. Wilberforce seemed aware of God's call and eager to serve: "My walk is a public one," he wrote in his diary. "My business is in the world, and I must mix in the assemblies of men or quit the post which Providence seems to have assigned me." He also increasingly felt the burden of his calling: "A man who acts from the principles I profess," he later wrote, "reflects that he is to give an account of his political conduct at the judgment seat of Christ."[5]

Wilberforce gave himself tirelessly to the work of abolition, and by the end of his life had cut a wide swath through the dense jungle of slavery. Refusing to turn a blind eye or to bask in personal comfort, he tackled his day's most obvious example of public injustice.[6]

Close on the heels of Wilberforce came another social reformer, Antony Ashley Cooper. This seventh Earl of Shaftesbury was, like Wilberforce, unable to stand by quietly while people suffered. He gave himself to the cause of the women and children regularly exploited by his society. As champion for the "ragged schools," the "climbing boys," lunatics, and factory workers, Shaftesbury rarely met a social cause he left untouched.

He served nearly sixty years in Parliament and together with other wealthy and influential Brits who formed the "Clapham Sect" set right numerous injustices. In 1846, he took a year off from government service to inspect firsthand lower-class neighborhoods. This led to improved sanitation for these communities. He was trusted implicitly because of the sincerity of his motives and methods; Shaftesbury once met with more than four hundred London thieves—at their invitation—and persuaded many to leave their life of crime.

Hannah More was another member of the Clapham Sect and is widely revered as the founder of the modern Sunday school movement. In the crushing poverty of London's slums, she found a group of people grossly burdened by illiteracy and disease; with education, she was able to improve their lot. She also illuminated their plight for many of the upper class.

Act justly. For people such as Wilberforce, Shaftesbury, and More, justice was more than a cozy discussion topic over mugs of cider by the fireplace: It was the very air they breathed, because of their commitment to God's goodness.

Love Mercy

"The LORD loves righteousness and justice" begins a couplet in Psalm 33. It concludes with "the earth is full of his unfailing love" (v. 5). The English "unfailing love" is a translation of the Hebrew noun *chesed,* which also means "mercy," as in Micah 6:8. *Mercy* is one of Scripture's big words. It covers the kindness of unfailing love; it also appears with a legal connotation, when someone pays for what another has done.

The two ideas come together in this way: You are in your father's car, one month after receiving your driver's license. You have been painstakingly careful in every excursion thus far, but today, as you are backing out, you hear the unmistakable scraping of metal. You leap from your vehicle and notice that the car parked behind you has a crumpled bumper and a mangled headlight. Your heart sinks, and you immediately begin calculating: Can I blame another? Can I rub out the dent with a rag? Can I avoid telling my dad? Can I afford this?

That last question sticks in your throat. You know that your bank balance is low; why else are you driving your parents' old beater? And you are pretty sure that neither parent will rush to bail you out of this mess. So you drive home, shaking, wondering what will happen. It doesn't take long to find out: As a new driver, the insurance company already considers you a high risk, so we won't be talking with them, your father states.

That leaves you and your sorry bank account. You stew for a day or so, while Dad tries to dicker with the owner of the other car. Nothing changes: She wants a new bumper. And then the unforeseen shows up. In the mail comes a letter from Grandma. You open it and remove a single page. It says, "I heard. Here." A second slip flutters into your lap. It's a check. All those zeroes, you think.

This is mercy: the kindness of unfailing love, the willingness to care for a wrong done by another. Grandma didn't wreck the car—you did. By rights, it should have been you who paid. But justice can be satisfied so long as there is atonement; with mercy, someone else can foot the bill.

You see the broader application. For God, justice must prevail. When sin occurs, it must be acknowledged and dealt with. At the same time, God values people; he doesn't want any of them to perish. When these people sin, as they do, justice requires payment. The only adequate payment is death, which puts God in a bind. He resolves the dilemma by permitting the satisfaction of justice with a special payment plan: Jesus comes—mercifully—to shoulder sin and die.

It's a wonderful arrangement that we willingly accept, until we hear Micah say, "love mercy." With this command, Micah is saying, be like God. Step in where you are able to pay for what has happened, to show kindness where it is needed, so that others might be preserved.

Wait a minute, we protest. It's one thing for me to receive mercy—but to show it? If I demonstrate mercy, that means I'll have to, you know, help someone who did something wrong, maybe even something wrong to *me!*

Exactly. This is the unmistakable force of mercy: It is personal. When we are kind, when we step in, when we move constructively into a situation where damage has occurred—particularly damage that has directly affected us—then we begin to grasp what it is that God wants from us.

Mercy does not keep an eye on the bottom line. It evaluates the present need and says yes. And here is what takes away all remaining breath: God doesn't stop with making payments with his priceless gift of Jesus. His mercy goes on, ready to fall on many more who need it. Despite their wanderings and rebellion, regardless of their hardness and smallness, God still wants people back. His mercy falls like rain on the just (of whom there are precious few) and the unjust. What makes it difficult to accept this is not that mercy *could* operate in satisfaction of justice, but thinking that it *would*.[7]

We are more inclined to seek revenge or demand payment, to insist that we be reimbursed for what has happened to us (with interest and extra for emotional distress added on). Love mercy. The command is so simple, so spare, so elegant, so unreachable. Is it possible? God shows that mercy is as real as sin. Its effect, however, is quite opposite. Where sin drains life, mercy restores it. When sin separates, mercy binds. What sin destroys, mercy rebuilds. Mercy preserves people's lives without compromising God's standards.[8]

A Testimony

The last epistle of the New Testament was written by Jude. Reliable tradition affirms that this man was the Judas mentioned in Matthew 13:55, who, together with James, was a half brother of Jesus. His brief letter—one of the "minor" epistles, perhaps—refers to mercy five times in the space of a single chapter.

Jude's interest in mercy is noteworthy because of what we know about him. He was, for instance, a detractor of Jesus early on. To be more precise, he thought Jesus was a lunatic (Mark 3:21). Then something happened, and Jude moved from critic to servant, from infidel to believer. Perhaps it was a personal appearance, such as his brother James experienced (1 Cor. 15:7). Maybe it was something less spectacular. Whatever the case, Jude switched sides.

Experience gave him special sensitivity to mercy. Imagine: You've grown up in the home of one you later accept as God's Messiah. Of course, early on, he was just your brother. Then he was just plain crazy. Did you tease him, taunt him, badger him—mercilessly? How did he respond? And then, when it dawned on you who he truly was, what happened? Were you filled with remorse? Did you wish you could replay those early years? Were you struck with fear at what God might do to you?

Then what happened? He does not treat you as your sins deserve.[9] You are welcomed by the church. You become a person of standing there, of influence. Your brother James goes on to lead the church of Jerusalem. People want to know what you think. God taps you as an author for his written revelation.

This enlarges your heart. It makes you prone to show mercy and to call for mercy from others. You speak from experience. You know what it's like to be a recipient of mercy, you who did nothing to deserve such good treatment but in fact truly deserved to be whomped by God. Your life will never be the same and neither, you hope, will the lives of those who hear what you have to say.

An Appropriate Use of Power

Justice and mercy make sense only in the context of power, which is a problem, because we often feel powerless.

Like the morning I sat in a restaurant booth waiting for a friend. I was reading a book, drinking coffee, and enjoying the peace. Then across from me, three people sat down: two straitlaced parents and their reluctant pierced and leathered daughter. The waitress came and received mumbled orders; when she retreated, the rumbling increased. "Why can't you . . . ?" the father demanded. "When will you . . . ?" the mother pleaded. The child sat, mashing a cloth napkin, steam rising through her darkened hair. "How come you never . . . ?" she snarled.

Their table conversation edged off a cliff into silence, and I drew further into my book. Helpless glances shot around their little triangle; eyes were clouded in anger and frustration. When the meal arrived, the clink of silverware against china was the only sound. Powerlessness oozed from that table like cold syrup over pancakes: Mom and Dad would have thrown up their hands, daughter would have stomped out exasperated had it not been so public a place. A short while later they left, business truncated, tempers leashed. But no good had come of their time together.

We face times such as these, when we stand like Scotty, calling up to the bridge: "I canna do it, Cahptin—we dinna haiv the powah." It's true, we convince ourselves we don't.

Really? Or is it more accurate to say that we have power but are unsure how to channel it? Or that we're like a teenager with a hot rod: We know what's under the hood but think only about the sounds and smells the engine can produce. In either case, we are irresponsible with the power that is available.

"His divine power has given us everything we need." Peter declares this reverently (2 Peter 1:3) on behalf of people he knows to be suffering because of their allegiance to Christ. Tell beleaguered men and women that they do, in fact, have power. What will be their likely response? So why does Peter take such an awful chance?

Over the course of a year I watched a friend build his house. I saw it in stages: a hole in the ground, floor joists, shingles on the roof. His son was an apprentice to an electrician, and on one trip to the site, I noticed that he had pulled wire through the studs. Outlets were in place, and light fixtures, but an extension cord still ran in from the house next door. On another visit, that snaking cord was gone. Lights shone and the outlets were hot; tools could be plugged in at the walls now because the house had been connected directly to the main at the street.

Peter knows that the people of God have ready access to God's power when he indwells them. Their houses are wired, so to speak, and once the Spirit comes, there is a connection with the main power grid. The really interesting question, of course, is, What is blocking that power's flow? A second is like it: What do you do with the power you have?

The first question resolves with prayer, honest examination, and repentance. The second is answered by Micah: Use power to act justly and to put mercy in play. The leaders of Micah's day had plenty of power that they used to trouble others. They were like a high school buddy who drove a GTO. He would stop by a house to pick up some kids, rev the engine in the patch of stones at the side of the yard, and scream at a parent as the last car door slammed, "Gotta rake?"

In the 1960s and 1970s, Latin America spawned various strains of liberation theology. Some versions tried to promote an end to poverty through violent revolution and were, accordingly, marginalized. But at a minimum, liberation theology forced us to reconsider the way we look at the poor and disadvantaged of our world. Is it right, these theologians ask, to support exploitation in any form? Can the church neglect those who live in economic and social distress? Is it not time for the church to direct her power appropriately, so that surplus flows toward need?

Power can spray debris, or cut another person in half, or shut out the sun's light and warmth as effectively as electric blinds. Or it can heal, help, promote, enrich. It depends on where we are in our walk with God.

Walk Humbly with God

It may be that you've grown accustomed to seeing God in the far distance, and you have to squint; he's so tiny as to be indistinct. Perhaps he is like a crack in the sidewalk outside your home: You know it's there and feel it when you ride your bike, but it is a relatively minor inconvenience and not a matter for losing sleep.

Micah pleads for a humble walk with God, which puts you in two places simultaneously. First, when you are humble, God is over you. Second, during your walk, he is with you. By seeing him over and with, you will not be so inclined to think yourself the center of life, nor will you imagine yourself cut off from support. From such a position, you find that acting justly and loving mercy actually become possible: You can draw on the strength of one superior to you and count on his encouragement as he moves alongside.

Humility is what God wants from his own, and those who discern this and practice humility find that he assists them. "God opposes the proud, but gives grace to the humble." Both James and Peter quote this saying from Proverbs 3:34 to make a point about submission. For Peter, the proverb directs people to be clothed with humility, as they consider others better than themselves (1 Peter 5:5–6). For James, the text is part of a diatribe that sounds downright prophetic as he castigates "adulterous people" who are moving toward "friendship with the world" (James 4:4). Where Jude appeals to mercy, his brother James hurls a warning about humility: "Submit . . . to God" (4:7). This is the only appropriate response of those who receive grace and those for whom God yearns (4:6).[10]

Who Is like God?

Justice. Mercy. Humility. The leaders of Micah's day had missed all three. As a result, they would soon be out—out of Israel and out of God's favor because of hearts closed off to him (Micah 6:10–16).

Power flows from God to people to be used wisely. "Does it make you a king to have more and more cedar? . . . Your eyes and your heart are set only on dishonest gain, on shedding innocent blood and on oppression and extortion." God spoke through Jeremiah (22:15, 17) to the son of Josiah, a worthless no-account named Shallum. Rather than following his estimable father's example, Shallum had struck his own path and faced God's fury. Shallum should have remembered what made Josiah great in God's eyes: "He defended the cause of the poor and needy" (Jer. 22:16). Instead, he abused the power he enjoyed as king.

Centuries later when Jesus broke on to the scene in Israel, he too would find the leaders of the day guilty of abusing the power with which they had been entrusted:

> Woe to you, teachers of the law and Pharisees, you hypocrites! You give a tenth of your spices—mint, dill and cummin. But you have neglected the more important matters of the law—justice, mercy and faithfulness. You should have practiced the latter, without neglecting the former.
>
> MATTHEW 23:23

God establishes what is good as a benchmark for people. When power is channeled such that this good occurs, God is pleased. If power is squandered by idolaters, God will be forced to make a correction. This is Jesus' point, and Micah's.

In Hebrew, Micah's name asks a question: Who is like God? It is a common question for prophets, asked in different ways of people who have forgotten about or rebelled against the Lord. Who is like God—"who pardons sin and forgives the transgression? . . . You do not stay angry forever but delight to show mercy. You will again have compassion. . . . You will be true. . . . and show mercy" (Micah 7:18–20)? Asherah, whose poles stab the countryside like needles; the Baals of the tolerated high places? Surely you jest.

Who is like God? It is a question leaders—be they kings, pastors, elders, Sunday school superintendents, general managers, floor nurses, parents, CEOs, deans, staff officers, or presidents—need to answer. Who is like God? You are, when you, like God, love to use your power for the benefit of others.

5

CHOOSE WISELY
Haggai

*W*e enter the world as regents, assuming others exist only to meet our needs and satisfy our whims. With time and a little sense, the baldness of this presumption gets a toupee of good manners, but in our hearts we barely change. Prophets speaking for God wield razors that shave pride to the nub and then tear at its roots. Pride cannot persist in the servant of God, they insist, and so we must give careful thought to our ways.

The prophets sound a lot like Solomon: "Trust in the LORD with all your heart and lean not on your own understanding; in all your ways acknowledge him, and he will make your paths straight" (Prov. 3:5–6). I found those verses years ago in the flyleaf of a Bible my parents gave me; the prophets would endorse them heartily, because following God's way means not persisting with pride or relying on luck, personal knowledge, or intuition. Following God means pursuing wisdom.

Wisdom—which, in the biblical lexicon, implies the application of God's will and ways to life—is foreign to human nature. Often, people prefer to stay fools, since foolishness is more natural and therefore easier. Wisdom is a decidedly more difficult row to hoe. It needs to be learned, apprehended, strapped on, and knit in so that life can count for something. It involves choice and discipline and delayed gratification, and that makes for a hard sell in any generation.

About four centuries after Solomon, Haggai stood in the tattered capital of Jerusalem to deliver his message. His listeners had recently returned from seventy years of exile far to the east of tiny Israel. Many of those who heard him would have been young people, Babylonian by birth, though Jewish by lineage. Nebuchadnezzar had taken their grandparents and parents from their homeland to live in Babylon until, decades later, Cyrus had set wheels in motion that allowed all who so wished to leave. Darius had done Cyrus one better by approving official resources for the temple's rebuilding back home.

Home? Home was Babylon, where so many of these people had been born or raised or lived the vast portion of their lives. Still, a large group became enthusiastic about the prospect, remembering, no doubt, stories about the Promised Land told by their ancestors. So many left—home—and headed west to a new land that had occupied the hearts and minds and lives of their forebears. They tramped through the desert for weeks and then finally crested the last hill, so that the fabled city of Jerusalem came into view. There it lay, as broken as after the Babylonians had descended and leveled the place seventy years before. Sure, property might be free, or part of a government-subsidized project, but it would be a long while before this place got to looking like home.

Can you feel the wind go out of their sails? Imagine a road trip with your family across country, back to the cottage where you spent summers as a kid. It has been passed on to you, the sole heir, and you're returning after a long hiatus to take possession. For years you've been telling your children tales of this place. Finally, they will get to see it!

You pull in, bone weary after long days in the van. Headlights cut through the drizzle at dusk, revealing an incomprehensible sight. What should have been a delightful chalet is now a charred mass. Only an old stone chimney stands erect. The foundation of blackened cinder blocks rims an uneven blanket of ash; small puddles of oily water fill depressions on the pocked floor. You sit in your seat, a hand on the wheel, open-mouthed. Your youngest asks, "Where is it, Daddy? Are we there yet?"

The Jews plodded back into a disheveled Jerusalem without fanfare. Eventually, the shock subsided, and they began to build. They needed homes to live in, shops to sell from, shelters for the vine keepers and pens for the shepherds. So they cleared ground, felled trees, stacked stone. With time and success and ease, the projects expanded: Simple dwellings grew larger, while new rooms grew ornate.

Into this building preoccupation Haggai strode with three messages from God in quick succession. The people's response is impressive: They pause, listen, and obey. But I am moving too fast here. We need more of the story and a closer look at Haggai's part in it.

We have Ezra to thank for background and detail. In the book bearing his name, we read how the story begins with Cyrus, king of Persia, who invites exiles of Israel to return home for the particular purpose of building a temple in Jerusalem. Many take him up on this offer and go, and work begins. But there is quick and fierce opposition to this building, and the project grinds to a halt. It is put on hold; blueprints sit on the shelf, gathering dust.

It is at this point that Haggai and another prophet—Zechariah—emerge. Their prophecies and assistance (see Ezra 5:1–2) encourage people to resume the temple project, which then rekindles opposition. But this time, the bad guys lose. Their complaints to Darius lead that ruler to check his records, where he finds that his predecessor Cyrus had not only encouraged the temple building but actually designated a portion of the royal treasury for the project. So Darius puts his stamp of approval on temple work and decrees that local revenues be made available for this purpose.

With money, official endorsement, and encouragement from two of God's recognized emissaries, the temple is quickly finished (Ezra

6:13–18). Celebrations are held, and temple ritual is reinstalled. But as subsequent history reveals, the temple's centrality quickly eroded. The exile had forced people to adapt their worship to local constraints, resulting in what would become the synagogue. Ironically, history attributes to Ezra and his contemporaries this development, which diminished the temple's importance. Along with this came the creation of a new class of religious experts, also attributed to Ezra, which would soon join the priestly class in Israel as arbiters, protectors, and promoters of the law.[1]

People Easily Distracted

Haggai occupies a hinge point in Jewish history. As one of the leaders coming out of the Babylonian exile, he stands at the threshold of a new era, when "business as usual" can no longer be carried out. An entire generation has grown up outside the Promised Land, and like Joshua of centuries past, Haggai will help to lead them back, to claim what God had given Abraham. There are some differences, of course: The people now are returning to a homeland, rather than occupying new territory; they set off with peaceable intentions.

There are also similarities to that earlier foray into Canaan: a new generation under seasoned, faithful leadership, an opportunity for a fresh start, a command from God to embark on their task. Notice too how this generation is distracted from its intended mission. Joshua's troops were supposed to conquer the land, but very quickly they succumbed to its enticements. These new returnees were supposed to rebuild the temple, but they are almost immediately snared by preoccupation with personal space.

So the prophet who helps to spark enthusiasm for going home brings a message of priorities: "Give careful thought to your ways," he says. "Choose wisely the course you will follow, because you are a people easily distracted."

Haggai could bring such a message to any of our faith communities and speak with similar confidence, because we still are people given to distraction. We start well enough but quickly fall prey to other things. We're "prone to wander," to quote Charles Wesley.

We're not bad, of course; the things that distract us aren't legally suspect or even morally questionable. But they are distractions that reroute mental acuity and bleed off energy that should be directed otherwise. This is why Haggai pleads, "Give careful thought to your ways." It is the recurring preface in his deliveries from God, and it ought to make us sit up and take notice.

Give Careful Thought to Your Ways

Careful thought has fallen out of vogue these days, according to the pundits who loudly herald its absence. Look at the banal programming on TV, the vapid lyrics of music, the falling scores on standardized exams, the short attention spans of our young, the insipid books and magazines being churned out, the trite- ness of political debates, they insist. Obvious, isn't it, that we are no longer thinking people?

Is it? How might one account for the avalanche of material being generated and displayed on the Internet? Why have so many new musicians recently tumbled onto the various charts? From where did these intricate, thought-provoking movies come? When has college enrollment been so high? Why are libraries more full than malls? Is it just the coffee that makes bookstores popular?

While some sectors can report a "dumbing down," there are many others in which levels of thinking are at an all-time high. This would suggest that the question should not be, Why aren't we thinking? but, What is the content and result of our thinking? Haggai's frequent encouragement (*five* times in the NIV transla- tion's two chapters) to "give careful thought to your ways" is not advocating an increase in philosophizing that makes thinking an end in itself. He wants, rather, for people to think carefully so that they will act well.

Give careful thought to your ways. Now, there is "way" as "man- ner," for the style of life to which one clings, and there is "way" as "path," for the road one follows in the course of daily life. The word, in both Hebrew and English, blurs two ideas, and God is concerned with each. The character of one's life along with the route one takes through it are both of interest to him. Do they captivate us as well?

Give careful thought to your ways. What we think about, then, is how we are moving through life. Often, our mental energy is consumed with the torrent of information that floods us daily. Many are buffeted, capsized, and even drowned by ever more turbulent data-streams. The web of a culture that prizes accomplishment and acquisition pulls people down, like the net shot at a fleeing lion that gradually brings the beast to the ground.

Funny: We who live in such cultures rarely notice their effect. We even find ourselves liking the webbing: "This color, texture—doesn't this look good on me?" we ask those around us who are similarly bedecked. "Sure," they reply. "More rope?"

We sneak a look into our neighbor's garage, scan on-line stores for the latest bauble, and secretly envy a coworker's zipper scar down the sternum that indicates the stress he's been under because of how hard he's worked. These glances occupy us so that we come to God preoccupied. The disciple's life is meant to steadily strip the detritus of culture that clamps on like barnacles below the waterline of a ship. We are not thinking carefully enough.

Here is a test. Ask: If I went to work tomorrow and learned I had been sacked, how would I evaluate my worth the next day? If I returned to my house after a vacation and found it sodden from a flash flood, what things inside it would I miss? If I had an afternoon without obligations, or found a thousand-dollar bill on the pavement, how would I spend it? My worth, my interests—to what are they tied? This stuff, these things—do they bring me closer to the Lord or distract me from him? Haggai's original listeners had to wrestle with such questions. So do we.

A church planter in Ireland teaches me about an uncluttered life. He begins each day with a long walk, during which he prays, listens, thinks. He is like Martin Luther, who found his days so busy that he could ill afford not taking the time to be quiet before God. He is like those who know the value of meditation and solitude; seasons of quiet are essential.[2]

This man lives austerely, the result of personal choice and calling. My own approach is less ascetic, but I have been challenged by him to reduce my accumulation of and dependence on stuff. It is this reduction of distraction that makes careful thinking more likely because now I have less to think about! Of course, if I steadily bemoan the lessening, I will quickly lose sight of its point and purpose, but if I can value a life uncluttered by things and events, I am likely to find my thinking becoming more productive.

With the prophet we must accord value to careful thought. We step away from machines, reduce "entertainment," question the need for what so many blithely accept as part of normal life. We routinely run an "introspective diagnostic," to gauge the condition of our heart, soul, and mind. We do this in quiet, seeking a refuge from the howling around us. As we do so, we discover what the psalmist expresses: God, you are my hiding place, my refuge (see, among several examples, Psalm 46). In this quiet place of refuge, we can be still—and know him more fully.

There is a connection between being still and knowing God. We fight this link—at least some of us do—telling ourselves rather that stillness is closer to indigence, indolence, indulgence. The prospect of time off, time away? Surely it is not for responsible people to shirk their responsibilities in favor of a break. Far better to press nose to grindstone. There are things to do! People to see! Houses to build!

Our nature slips into this gear readily. We move so fast from the need of a shelter to the longing for a showplace that we are hardly aware of the time lapsed or the money spent. Haggai saw this clearly and used the houses around him as object lessons. Sporting accoutrements like paneling (Hag. 1:4), these houses had gone past what was necessary into what was conspicuous. The problem was not luxury itself—stories about Daniel, David, Barnabas, and others should persuade us that God is not uniformly opposed to wealth. The problem was that the interest in decoration had distracted the people from their first priority: They had come to build a temple.

Those who fail to pay attention become victims of distraction. Sometimes distractions emerge from sources we might otherwise judge to be good or benign. A family, for instance: Is it wrong to build a house for one's family? Scripture teaches that when one begins, in God's will, to form a family, there come certain responsibilities. From Jesus we also hear the counterpoint:

> If anyone comes to me and does not hate his father and mother, his wife and children, his brothers and sisters—yes, even his own life—he cannot be my disciple. And anyone who does not carry his cross and follow me cannot be my disciple.

LUKE 14:26–27

We may soften the blow of his words, tempering "hate" to a more palatable phrase, but we must not be blind to the lurking danger: A family can also distract one from continuing to pursue God's will. Haggai's warning exposed this problem. The prophet clearly saw how houses under construction ostensibly for various families had begun to consume people so that they lost interest in other pursuits. Their problem was not so much a result of loving family as of leaving God.

Give careful thought to your ways. This means take care. Grow quiet. Be still. Only then can the mind be actively engaged and sufficiently alert to whatever might pull one off God's way. To put the matter in other terms, this is why self-discipline—the willful decision to say no to self and yes to God—is so important. Lives governed by such discipline tend to stray from God's way less often, because they are often sticking a wet finger up for the blowing of the Spirit rather than holding the wheel of their own destiny in a death grip.

Discipline. We associate the term with the regimen of a concert pianist who spends hours every day practicing scales. Or it rings of punishment and conjures images of boarding school or unbridled parents. But think instead of the word on which "discipline" is built: *disciple*. Discipline is what a disciple manifests to be an effective follower of Christ. When heart, soul, and mind are centered on an obedience of God fueled by love for God, then the disciple makes progress. Discipline is essential to discipleship.

This is the point Jesus wanted to make as he walked among people, calling them to abandon self in favor of following God. This is the prophet's charge too: A person must exercise discipline while walking along God's way. The careful, thoughtful choice to pry fingers off one's life so that God may assume sovereignty is what prepares a person for progress. It is a steady battle, joined on open fields and in dark corners, where God, the Lord Almighty, fights with and for us.

He Is the LORD Almighty

In a book of only two chapters, certain phrases are notable for their repetition. One is "give careful thought to your ways." A second is Haggai's name for God: the LORD Almighty. Literally, the Hebrew reads, "God of Armies." "Armies" was later smoothed by English translators to "Hosts," which speaks of the large number of soldiers under a military leader's command. "Host" is not often used in this way in contemporary vocabulary, so the term gets further buffing. "Almighty" conveys the sense of the word in a way we can grasp: The one who leads a large, strong group is himself estimable; if the group is bigger and stronger than any other, this leader is All-mighty.[3]

Remember that Haggai is addressing people who, for the most part, have been raised under the imperial system of Babylon and/or Persia. They could easily have been influenced by contemporary thought that elevated the current king or emperor to near-divine status, and so they needed a firm reminder that God was above all and truly the most mighty. Haggai's use of this name for God reminds listeners that their God is far greater than a Darius, Cyrus, or Nebuchadnezzar.

There is a second implication in this name. Darius, Cyrus, Nebuchadnezzar—as impressive as these men were—were not the only contenders for the crown. Perhaps the most significant threat to God's status was each person's own heart. After all, those kings could control only one's environment; the keys to a heart are individually held. So here is a second reason why Haggai speaks of the "LORD Almighty": He wants to convince his listeners that God should have priority not only over kingdoms and world powers but also over one's own agenda.

But wait, the thoughtful person avers. Is this what God is after—control? Does God seek to dominate to the point that a person loses individuality and blindly accedes to his demands? No. God could easily rewire us as robots; some might suggest that to do so would be far more efficient. But his commitment to the full implications of love assures freedom and choice.

Those who in love obey him discover no end of trouble. Self, accustomed to the addictive sweetness of disobedience, is reluctant to let go. The enemy, opposed to all that smacks of God, can be fierce. Prophets know this struggle, understand its nature, empathize with its intensity, earnestly hope for victory. This explains a third reason why Haggai designates God the way he does: The LORD Almighty comes to fight alongside his disciples and for them.

I Am with You

A third phrase Haggai repeats is this promise: "I am with you" (1:13; 2:4). Remarkably, prophets who bring harsh words also include tender reminders such as this, assuring people that the God who so strongly insists on obedience and repentance from his people also longs to enjoy peaceful fellowship with his people. The God who calls for a hard thing intends to stand alongside those who plan to attempt it.

We lived for a long time in the age of heroes, those rugged individuals who broke new ground, single-handedly, by their daring exploits. These days, we tend much more to emphasize teams. So we do not hear of a single astronaut bravely orbiting the earth but of those who helped him break free of gravity's pull, stay aloft, and be pulled safely from the sea. Rare are the management executives whose solo efforts reform a company; rather, there is a group that shared responsibility for the turnaround. The athlete who sets a new world record? It happened with the help of trainers, dieticians, masseuses, and corporate sponsors. Same for the movie star, who couldn't stand on this podium tonight if it weren't for . . .

God is interested in teamwork too. In the words of the preacher, "Though one may be overpowered, two can defend themselves. A cord of three strands is not quickly broken" (Eccles. 4:12). God invites a person to walk a new path, one different from that insisted on by self. He also promises to be a steady companion along this new way, no matter where the road leads.

I am with you. When you walk away from the familiar terrain mapped by self, the path quickly takes on a new character. At times, this new way is delightful, and we can affirm with the psalmist that "the boundary lines have fallen for me in pleasant places" (Ps. 16:6). At other times, however, the going is rough, and we find ourselves in the shadows of a box canyon. In times such as these, we are prone to worry, to curl up and whimper, or to rail at the high walls. But even here, God is present (Ps. 23:4).

As we consider God's role for the present, there is hardly a more potent promise than this. But it is precisely this promise that we are prone to doubt, because we find our selves easily threatened, and we do not like that feeling. So we strike out at God, the one we thought would make it all better, and we lean back toward self, knowing how good we can be to ourselves.

There are two possibilities when we face threats to self: We can cling to God, or we can abandon him. He will not leave us; he has promised as much. But neither will he force us to hold on. The prophets, after all, spent much of their energy speaking exactly to those who at one time had a firm grip on God but then, on account of various events, influences, and circumstances, had loosened it. Come back, they cry. Remember, God is with you.

If God is with you, you can build with abandon. You can abandon the demands of self to pursue the will of God. You can do this with assurance that what you are doing is significant and worthwhile, with confidence that you have another nearby applying himself to the work, and with delight in being near one who loves you so much.[4] God partners with you in the labor of rebuilding a self, in the effort of a new journey. You are not on the job site by yourself; there is a powerful helper nearby. You are not riding solo cross-country; you are part of a team that wants you to succeed.

Think of a marriage. When the bride stands before a group of friends, family, and assorted well-wishers to say her vows, the marriage has only begun. She will not wake the next day to continue the routine that to this point has revolved around her own needs and desires; she starts this day in a new state. There is another in her life now, and for the rest of her life she will seek to meld with this person. She does not relinquish her self in this melding; two individuals still compose any marriage. But she forgoes the demands that her self is inclined to make; she submits for the sake of love. And she depends on this other for help, encouragement, and support in the ongoing work of submission.

Now, here is the glorious mystery that emerges from a successful marriage: With a commitment to submission, the result is health, not misery. We might think that self would become so submerged in the other that only a shell would remain. But this is not the case at all. Instead, the baser instincts are rooted out in the process of submission, shriveled by the bright light of love.

The choice to follow God's way cannot be made in the power of self alone. We are not strong enough for that. It can happen only when we commit to love and agree to receive assistance. So notice, God will send his messenger to urge that the choice of a new path be taken, but he is quick to add that he intends to undertake the journey as well. We go together, aided by God himself.

Holiness Is a Joint Venture

Haggai's listeners got it. "They came and began to work on the house of the LORD Almighty" (1:14). According to Ezra (5:2), Haggai, along with a fellow prophet Zechariah, joined in the labor to produce a structure that would later resound with God's glory (Hag. 2:7). Such a promise would lift the heads and quicken the steps of workers; they could imagine a day when God himself would inhabit the place they had built. But there was still the matter of a lingering, threatening mind-set.

"Ask the priests what the law says" (Hag. 2:11). With this instruction God begins to tear away at a damaging misperception. According to accepted interpretations of the law, holiness was nontransferable, protected by a sort of invisible firewall that kept it from affecting anything down the line. Defilement, on the other hand, was different. Its contagion could spread like chicken pox in a church nursery. Why did either of these points matter? For this reason: If you are raised in a system that prizes holiness,[5] you find yourself very quickly in a bind. Not only is that standard put steadily before you, but you soon learn from experience that you cannot hope to reach it. The bar is not forever being raised just as you approach it; it was placed so high initially that no leap could ever come close.

On the other hand, non-holiness is lurking at every turn. Each day you run the very real risk of defiling yourself in a host of known and unknown ways. Your travels, diet, and interactions, to name just a few, are fertile hotbeds of trouble, and you can barely escape a day in the marketplace without encountering some threat to your ritual purity. This is why Pharisees were forever washing themselves. Indeed, this is why Pharisees constructed such an elaborate system of "hedging" the law: They feared breaking it, and thus incurring defilement, if they ever flagged in their diligence at keeping it.

If you are raised in such a tense atmosphere—the tension caused by knowing you can not measure up and are likely to fall even further behind just in the normal course of living—what impact would that have on your self-image? What might it produce in the community of which you are a part? Can you begin to sense why legalists and libertines[6] emerged so rapidly in the culture of that day?

Through Haggai, God is challenging common misperceptions such as these. True, as he acknowledges, the law does lean in particular ways when it comes to holiness and defilement. But why? Is the intent of the law to produce neuroses—to introduce people to a system they cannot hope to keep or to remind them of their constant shortcomings? Of course not. The purpose of the law is to lead people to God.[7] Too often the law was seen as an end in itself; God emphasizes rather that it is a vehicle by which people can come to him.

In this case, the law teaches that God has standards regarding holiness and its opposite. God's will for people is holiness, a point he makes often and in various ways, but just as quickly, God stresses that the pursuit of holiness is a joint venture. When a person is joined by—partners with—God's Holy Spirit, holiness is a likely outcome.

One of the Spirit's missions will be to help people overcome the tendency to cling to false concepts. This is why God delivers through Haggai a word about defilement and holiness: The people listening need to release their grip on the notion that all they do is bad and wrong and that becoming attractive to God is impossible. In this, too, careful thinking is essential.

If God is for them—if, as he has said, he is *with* them—then success in God's estimation is possible. The message he brings is this: By choosing to focus on the temple, you have shown a willingness to obey that puts you firmly in my camp. Therefore, I am with you, and because of that you can, with the continued assistance of the Spirit who "remains among you" (Hag. 2:5), be holy. You can take the path that leads toward submission and simplicity.

God's Way

On a sunny day in La Dehesa, one of the suburban *communas* outside Chile's capital, Santiago, gliders float gently in the blue sky. From the ground, they seem idyllic, pockets of quiet removed from the bustle of a crowded city. My friend Rick flew in a glider and explained how they work.

You arrive early at the airport to be strapped in behind a pilot who will navigate the craft. A tow cable attached to the glider's nose allows a small prop plane to take you high. From inside the glider, you pull a release lever, and you are free to float. The key to a long ride is finding updrafts.

Updrafts are common in hilly terrain, especially when the air is hot and dry. This is why gliders favor Santiago: A desert climate and location at the base of the Andes make the area ideal for their sport. Small, puffy clouds signal the presence of updrafts, and pilots look for and steer toward them. When pilots reach a cloud, they tip a wing into the column of warm air and aim the plane at the ground. The move is counter-intuitive, and its resulting downward corkscrew appears to the novice like the plunge of death.

Then the unexpected occurs. The plane begins to rise, pushed by a current of warm air. In fact, the force of this air rushing up from the surface is sufficient to lift the plane even higher, such that it is able to break free from this updraft and coast to the next thermal, farther away. In this manner, a glider can remain aloft for hours and cover hundreds of miles.

When we begin the journey that is our life, we do so believing that we sit at the controls of a 767. All we need to do, we reason, is to start the engines, push the throttle forward, and scream down the runway. In no time, we will lift off, achieve cruising altitude, and steer toward our chosen destination.

God's way is more like piloting a glider. One must count on exterior, unseen forces, and one must go down in order to go up. Going down is the work of discipline, choosing to say no to self and yes to God. Outside help comes from the Spirit, who, though unseen, provides needed power for the trip.

There is a partnership as two distinct entities meld for the purpose of pleasing God. While this partnership is not quite symbiotic, the one never belittles the other for lacking power. Rather, God delights to offer what is needed and works as the person gives him room to operate. God's empowering presence is never absent, except when the person decides to turn out of the warm updraft to attempt self-powered flight. That trip, of course, is brief and precarious.

The Promise of Reward

Prophets urge people to come near and stay close to God and to be about his business. "Be strong . . . and work" Haggai enjoins (2:4); stay focused on what is before you, and don't let anything distract you from the task at hand. Teachers do the same, urging a class of fifth graders to stay "on task." Why? Because fifth graders are a squirrelly lot, quick to yank a pigtail, or upset a paint tray, or drop a pencil, or snicker at a joke. A thousand things crowd the classroom each day and threaten the teacher's agenda, so he must be alert.

Punishment is not enough. It can get a student's attention—much as God's withholding of rain (Hag. 1:10) or his bringing of blight, mildew, and hail (2:17) was designed to garner attention—but punishment alone is not the hallmark of a good teacher. Encouragement must flow and with it the promise of reward for accomplishing the task.

Why does the teacher call a student to perform—for his own good, or the student's? What teacher needs the math or artwork of a ten-year-old? But what teacher does not rejoice when the student answers properly and draws well?

This rejoicing is a signal that the work has been mastered, the task completed, the lesson learned. Now the student can progress to another task, a new job. The process does not stop with a success because it is a journey and not simply a test. As the student learns, the teacher can add more, not to frustrate the student but to increase education.

"From this day on I will bless you" (Hag. 2:19). God promises reward because he sees in these people a heart committed to him. Previously, they were self-interested and self-consumed, but lately that has changed. They have left behind the wallpaper books and fabric swatches and carpet samples and paint chips to gather for a project that has lasting value: building a temple. As impressive as this engineering feat is, however, the real work is not about bricks, mortar, and timber from the mountains. What the temple construction project indicates is this: a people willing to choose God's way over their own.

The Life of Discipleship

Going down in order to rise is the way of discipleship and the sort of life produced by the discipline rendered from careful thinking. Jesus advocated this way during a lengthy exchange with disciples, opponents, and onlookers that Luke recorded (chaps. 14–18 of that Gospel). All manner of objections were raised; Jesus stood his ground. There are other ways, he freely acknowledged, but none of them will land one in the kingdom of God.

Disciples of God are people comfortable with loss. They forego reputation and expectation; they are forever clearing out time and space. In place of these, they cultivate Simone Weil's "decreation,"[8] saying no to themselves—and yes to God. There is about them a profound sense of loss, because they are people who hold virtually nothing dear. As Peter says, only a few things truly matter: "We have left all we had to follow you" (Luke 18:28).

It is not a boast so much as a statement of fact. Paul would later say that all they had left behind was inconsequential. Worse than that, actually. Paul likened his own accomplishments and laurels to the stuff we leave on the curb for the garbage collectors or, to be more precise, the stuff we remove from the horse barns (Phil. 3:7–8).

To consider everything a loss (Phil. 3:7)—what does this take? The careful thought of a Spirit-ordered mind, which in wisdom exchanges the fleeting kudos of material life for a long-lasting knowledge of and experience with Christ. This is what the disciple yearns for, what discipline produces. And in the end, the loss is not counted. One's personal balance sheet does not become acceptable because it shows a greater number of credits than debits in the life with God; the debit side of the sheet is blank, all "losses" having been absorbed by faith in a present, powerful God. It's a radical accounting procedure, beyond the grasp of any who insist on living large.

Haggai called people to leave their homes for God's house. Jesus said (in Luke 18:29–30) that no one who left a house—or a parent, sibling, or child, for that matter—would come up short. Those words of his followed an interview with the rich ruler, whom we remember as one whose wealth kept him from God. But what Jesus wants us to see here is that it was not the young man's money but his life that pushed God out to arm's length. A large bank account is no inherent problem; a heart closed off by and insulated with money is.

Once disciples make the shift in mind, heart, and soul—once they discipline themselves to follow through on God's bidding—then they can be devoted to God. He comes swiftly: "From this day on I will bless you," he promises (Hag. 2:19). And the blessings flow—blessings that matter not to the bottom line but at the bottom of a new heart and in the center of a wise mind.

6

BE COURAGEOUS
Amos

A friend once prayed for me, "Lord, right now Dan has no idea what he should do. Please give him the wisdom you promise." I winced at the observation that I had reached the end of my rope but couldn't argue with this guy's conclusions. Sometimes we need wisdom. We need to think carefully and well about what God has to say about situations we face.

And sometimes we need courage. We know what we ought to do but need the moxie to put hands and feet to that understanding. We need courage, but we feel fear. We are afraid that what we say or do might be misperceived. We are concerned that if we come out of the shadows, we will suddenly be exposed. We are paralyzed: What if I'm wrong? What if I'm right?

So much to fear. This is one reason why we are drawn to stories of courage and valor: We want those heroes to infuse us with boldness and resolve. We know that we are weak-willed and inadequate so often; we tremble much. One man described a walk with his young daughter one evening. She noticed her shadow for the first time. It scared her, and she ran.

The story makes us chuckle, nervously. We may not be scared of our own shadow, but walk down a cinder road through a forest on a cloudy night. How does it feel? Drive with traffic along a busy interstate and hear your front left tire blow out. How does it feel? Dial up your on-line broker and notice that your stock just fell 30 percent. How does it feel? Prepare to confront someone who's done something wrong. How does it feel? The fear that fills our hearts with that fetid vapor is ancient, pervasive.

So much to fear, even for people of faith.

Fear the Right Thing

Amos helps us put fear in its place. He knows what it is to be afraid, but he also helps us grasp the good fear can accomplish. For this bold prophet, fear—specifically the fear of God—is the foundation of courage.

The fear of God? This means "respect," right? Just as we should respect people, so we should have a healthy respect for God. True. God deserves our respect. But fearing God means more than this. Listen to Amos's metaphor as he talks about his own experience with God: "The lion has roared—who will not fear?" (3:8). Does a lion produce respect? Perhaps—but what's a more natural understanding? Fear.

Amos is one of the first biblical figures to compare God to a lion. Some in Scripture use lions as symbols of power and majesty, roaming the forest and field, taking what they want when they please. Occasionally, they are employed figuratively, as part of a prophet's vision or as metaphors for some particularly impressive people. But Amos, like Job (10:16) and Isaiah (31:4), pictures *God* as a lion. This keeps us from making him too cozy and forces us to sit up and take notice. The image lingers: John, for instance, will recycle it in Revelation, where Jesus is the triumphant Lion of Judah (Rev. 5:5). C. S. Lewis is a well-known example of subsequent writers who adopted this metaphor.

Lions give us a good feel for fear. Imagine not a pacified lion in some city zoo, fat and happy in the sun, but the wild variety—enormous, unpredictable, powerful. Now imagine this beast springing out of the high grass as you walk a ragged path. The creature pauses, vast yellow eyes glittering. Your heart rate doubles. As the lion reveals gleaming teeth in a mouth the size of your head, his bellow shakes every nearby tree. What is happening inside you right now?

Lewis scolds us in his Narnia Chronicles, assuring us that Aslan, his key figure, is not a "safe" lion. Amos knows that this is a lion whose roar shakes foundations, upsetting the comfortably balanced life. This lion should make us afraid.

But does it? Or do we prefer our lions fenced, or remote, roaming far away in deep, dark Africa?

Amos will have none of this. For him, the lion's roar snaps the bars of any cage. Faced with this lion, Amos goes down flat. He would pull us down there with him too, because we are a people not prone to fear God. Respect, sure; reverence even. But fear? That's not often found in our vocabulary. It is not that we are wonderfully courageous; in fact, we fear much. It is simply that too often we lack the wisdom to fear the right thing.

Fear Can Be a Good Thing

As a teenager, I spent a weekend on an outlying island with a church group. At the end of our time, some friends and I decided to take our two small powerboats back to the large island using the water instead of trailers. We left early because of a weather report we caught on the radio.

Part way home, I glanced over my shoulder. The sky behind me had grown ominously dark. I looked harder. In the distance I could see a long, narrow funnel connecting sea and sky: a waterspout. We had known trouble was coming and had left early enough to avoid it. Or so we had thought. The storm was upon us now.

We notched the throttles forward and pounded across waves whipped by increased wind. We strained to see our home jetty ahead and then looked back to track the waterspout's progress. And we sang. Beatles' songs as I recall, at the top of our lungs. Because we were invincible that day. We could outrun, outmaneuver, outthink, outlast any threat. A storm? Hah! We roared across that choppy sea, determined to win the race. We did. Our jetty appeared in the mist; we turned toward it and sped in, safe, protected, exultant. We had won.

We were fools.

Waterspouts kill people. These seaborn tornadoes can easily pluck a boat from the waves and spill it or push it far below the surface; we could have died that day. We heard the reports, knew what danger was brewing, but we sallied forth, oblivious. No, not exactly. We went because we thought ourselves stronger, better, smarter, impervious. A storm might upset others, but not us. We had plans, and getting swamped by a storm was not among them.

We should have been more careful. More fearful.

Jon Krakauer makes a convincing case that the main reason more than a dozen people died attempting to summit Mount Everest in 1996 was a lack of fear.[1] The drive for notoriety, cockiness based on previous experience, ineptitude, and poor conditioning all contributed to disaster for various individuals, but the common thread was a lack of fear: Too many refused to be afraid of that mountain, and as a result, many died.

Some fear is good. This is why, when I stand with my daughters on a gravel path high above the rocky Pacific coast, I speak a stern word. Finally, I have been sufficiently impressed by danger that I can be moved by fear. It is a fear I want to share with others, so I talk with my kids, trying to set fear into their young hearts before they scamper to the edge of an enormous boulder perched precariously a dozen meters above a treacherous beach.

Fear can perform a good work. It need not keep us from activity; just because we are afraid, we do not necessarily freeze in our tracks. But neither do we press on blithely. We move, in fear, focused.

The Fear of God

The lion has roared. This fear-inspiring sound did not debilitate Amos. As the developing story shows, the lion's roar instilled a new level of courage, helped him focus on the essentials. When you square off with a lion, your mind is, at that moment, wonderfully clear of distraction.

This is why we must be careful not to settle only for "respect." While there is in this notion some of what "fear" entails, "respect" is not a big enough basket to hold all the implications. When the Bible says we are to fear God, it means, listen to that roar, and let it knock you down.

To be candid, fear is no stranger to us. We fear, for instance, people. We fear that they will notice us or ignore us; we fear that they will belittle or misunderstand. We fear that we will not please them, or that we will be used by them, or that they will not appreciate us or will run over us. We fear being overlooked; we fear not fitting in. We fear abandonment; we fear smothering. This snarl of conflicting urges and hopes results in a tangle of fear that wraps us tight and wears us down.

Is *this* what it means to fear God? No. There is a fundamental difference between debilitating and constructive fear. The fear of people ensnares (see Prov. 29:25). The fear of God is the beginning of wisdom (Prov. 1:7; 9:10; 15:33), wisdom that opens us to careful, creative, empowering thinking and behavior. The fear of God prolongs life (Prov. 10:27; 14:27; 19:23); the fear of God is the key to delight (Isa. 11:3; 33:6). We are so accustomed to being enslaved by our fear of others that we have not stopped to consider that fear may actually be beneficial. Fear can help us focus, clearing out what distracts us so that we are wholly occupied by what matters.

Take the electrician wiring the panel for a new home. He can stand there before the many cables thinking, *There's enough voltage here to scramble my brains for a few days or even to kill me. Do I really want to do this?* Or he can study the layout, think carefully, and deliberately connect the conduit properly. His fear of the power of electricity will make him an effective electrician.

The Foolish

The lion has roared. This focuses Amos for delivering God's message, regardless of its content or the way its delivery may rebound negatively on the messenger. With a properly grounded fear of God, he will be courageous and not easily snared by those mortals around him.

His message begins with a roar (1:2) as Amos wades among Israel's neighbors with the announcement of God's extreme displeasure. Damascus, Gaza, Tyre, Edom, Ammon, and Moab are all chastised for their inhumane treatment of various people groups. The Jews know these neighbors and have felt the lash of their cruelty more than once. A stinging rebuke from Amos was guaranteed to prompt a chorus of strong approval. It was also an effective way to gather a crowd.

So imagine the reaction when Amos turned his gaze away from surrounding tribes toward the homeland. First under the knife was Judah. By this time[2] the nation had been divided for nearly 150 years. Israel, with its capital of Samaria, occupied most of the land, while Judah, whose capital was Jerusalem, encompassed a much smaller portion in the south. Amos came from Judah, according to his autobiographical introduction, but his public impact was in the north, in Israel.

Judah's censure (2:4) would have met with hearty agreement in Israel. Those southerners deserved, so their northern relatives surely thought, the flames of judgment God was promising (2:5). What a great day this was for Israel: First, all those idiots in neighboring countries are finally pegged for judgment by God, and now, Judah gets pounded. Delicious!

But Amos's work is not done until the finger of justice points at Israel. The remainder of chapter 2—a portion nearly twice as long as the denunciation of any other group—is occupied with God's assessment of Israel. Their greed, blasphemy, and callous indifference to the plight of the poor are more than enough to guarantee a harsh sentence.

Instead of developing a healthy fear for God, the leaders of Amos's day had pursued their own interests to the point of abusing other people. They easily forgot the many evidences of God's miraculous care (2:10) and brazenly abused the very agents he sent (2:12); for these reasons, they were under indictment. Their foolishness was all the more blatant when seen in light of the lengths to which God went to draw them to himself.

"You only have I chosen" (3:2). Perhaps Israel's greatest sin was indifference. God had reached toward them, showering them with gifts, extending to them grace. In response, they had turned away, drawn by the flash and glitter of fool's gold. Put a toddler in a high chair and offer her a neatly folded thousand-dollar bill with one hand and a large cone of chocolate ice cream with the other. Which will she choose? The wrong one, every time. So it was with Israel: They repeatedly spurned the valuable love of God.

Even when God changed tactics, they failed to respond. He could hold back food and water (4:6–7), and still they refused to acknowledge him. He could bring sickness, difficulty, and even death, all to no avail. On account of that hardness, that aloofness, Israel was doomed (5:2). And yet . . . the God whose sense of justice is mightily offended by hard hearts retains within himself a vein of mercy that cannot be exhausted. "Seek me and live," he promises (5:4), holding out an olive branch. There was still hope.

Three times he repeats the promise (5:4, 6, 14), but in the end he knows that they will refuse. So he turns to the final page, for a description of what they can expect. It is the coming "day of the Lord" (5:18), a time when God will unleash the full extent of his fury against all who have ignored or blasphemed him by following substitutes. It is a terrible day, one that he does not wish on any. But it is an inevitable day also, destined to roll down on the recalcitrant like a mighty river (5:24). As a prelude, these people will be carried off in exile (5:27).

Amos's message winds around a single stake: These people are indifferent to God. They "are complacent," "lie on beds," "lounge," "strum," and "drink wine" (6:1–6), all activities characteristic of people governed only by personal desire. And all of it ensures God's wrath: "I abhor the pride of Jacob" (6:8). Interesting phrase, this last one.

The Lion's Roar

Jacob was one of the early patriarchs, the grandson of Abraham, to whom God had made promises about both land and progeny. Jacob wrestled with God, following a twenty-year stay outside that Promised Land and just prior to reentry—the match ended in a draw and Jacob was renamed "Israel" (see Genesis 32). The "pride of Jacob"? No doubt it developed subtly, its seeds planted in the heart of one who wrestled with God and did not flag. Jacob was a guy who made his own way: When he wanted something, he went after it. Yes, he trusted God, but as you read the stories you sense an uneasy alliance, because Jacob also tended to rely on his own native abilities.

He had met his match in an equally crafty Laban, the father of Jacob's wife Rachel. Exasperated by Laban's poor treatment, Jacob had finally left his in-laws to return to Canaan. The parting of these two was marked by a rancorous exchange, which is notable, given our present interest, for a comment Jacob made. It is Jacob's reference to God that intrigues, because Jacob called him "the Fear of Isaac" (in Gen. 31:42, 53).

Curious. This one for whom pride would become a distinguishing character trait recalls a name his father had for God— a name that focused on fear. Fear of Isaac—of all things, why call God this? Could it be that Isaac—whom we meet as the miraculous answer to God's preposterous promise that Abraham and Sarah will have a child, only to be selected by God as a sacrifice some years later—had a special understanding of God? That Isaac realized, having been face-to-face with death at God's hand, so to speak, that he was not someone to mess with? That God was, properly, one who warrants fear?

What Isaac knew, Jacob only remembered. And what Jacob remembered, his descendants forgot. They were of the opinion that God was convenient—good for discussing at holidays, helpful if the water got a bit deep—but not really all that important in a daily way. For them God easily became a nuisance, interrupting the good life, the wine and roses, the feasting and the lounging. They had forsaken the wisdom of fearing him.

So God stepped in, roaring like a lion, intending to "smash the great house into pieces" (6:11). In preparation, he provides Amos with a sneak preview: three visions of the judgment about to fall. This coming destruction evokes Amos's compassion, and the prophet leaps into the gap between a holy God and errant people. "Sovereign LORD, forgive! How can Jacob survive?" (7:2). This happens twice: God predicts judgment; Amos begs leniency. Twice God relents, attentive to the prophet's pleas. But there is a third vision of a plumb line (7:8), and Amos, recognizing the trend, realizing that the people truly are hard-hearted, offers no mitigating word. "I will spare them no longer" (7:8), God promises.

There is a pause in the action as the visions fade and Amos encounters Amaziah, a court priest and official of King Jeroboam, who represents the popular attitude. He cannot stand for Amos's harsh invectives and tries to dissuade the prophet from continued activity. "Go back home," he counsels (7:12); "speak the words you have to Judah instead, and leave us in peace. You have no place in this king's realm, and you are not welcome."

Amaziah stares over Amos's shoulder and sees the storm clouds brewing, but he could care less. We can beat this so-called prophet, he thinks to himself. He has no fear of the God whose words Amos brings. He is a fool.

Amaziah's foolishness is evident in several ways. First, because he made no effort to determine whether Amos truly spoke for God. Second, because he considered the king's role and comfort superior to that of God's. And third, because he confused Bethel with what constituted true worship.[3] All this shows a profound lack of concern for God, and when God is devalued, people are not far behind. This is why Amaziah can turn a blind eye to societal inequities and be so cavalier toward Amos. If the God in whose name Amos speaks has little cachet for Amaziah, then only Amos's social standing is of consequence. And priests trump shepherds any day.

Amaziah held all the cards: He was the king's agent in Bethel and leader of the religious center of Israel. He had a wealth of tradition and public opinion on his side; he stood for the establishment and the right way of doing things. Unfazed, Amos digs in his heels: "I was neither a prophet nor a prophet's son, but I was a shepherd, and I also took care of sycamore-fig trees. But the LORD took me . . ." (7:14–15).

So much courage in this prophet, and now we understand its source. Amos recalls his own experience, when the lion's roar first shook him to the core. Up to that point he had been content with raising sheep and tending trees, but when God thundered, Amos had no choice other than to respond. Called into a completely new profession, thrust out of the orchard and away from the pasture into the press of hostile crowds, Amos does not shrink back from delivering the hard word. Even when he stands toe to toe with Amaziah, Amos has no fear.

Because he fears God. He has been thrown to his knees, knocked to his senses, and all he can hear is God's voice ringing in his ears. Like Moses, he had been occupied with sheep in some remote area; like Moses, that ended abruptly with a call from God that changed him irrevocably (3:8). Amos can now no more ignore the call of God than he can watch a lamb be mauled by a bear. When God calls, he answers.

It is this call from God that radically reorients Amos's world. It plunges him deep into the life of devotion to God, to the point that he will walk away from a satisfactory career and begin what is guaranteed to produce hard times.[4] Remarkably, we can detect no hint of regret. We never find Amos moaning about the life he now has, never hear him pining away for his hut on the hill back home. Such complaining is part of the biblical corpus elsewhere—had Amos done so, we would know—but the text is silent here. Except for Amos's resolute delivery of hard words.

God took me, he says. This life-changing action gave Amos a star to steer by and kept him from looking back.[5] When the lion roars, you hear it, and if you are wise enough, it strikes fear into your heart—fear that gives you a wonderful clarity about what really matters. Notice the progression: Wisdom begets fear, which then begets more wisdom. And courage. And action.

The threats of Amaziah? Incidental. A person anchored to popular opinion would have shriveled at the critique of the court priest, but Amos stands tall. Go back? Unthinkable. You sense the steel in the sound of Amos's retort: "Now then, hear the word of the LORD" (7:16).

Healthy Fear

We cannot stop with or be confused by "natural" fear. There is, for instance, the natural fear that rises whenever our life—or even our way of life—is threatened. Some anger, resentment, or frustration might blend in as well, but fear routinely appears. Left unchecked, this fear can debilitate: You can freeze climbing the icy side of a mountain face; you can stop thinking when you hear a strange sound downstairs; you can withdraw when another yells cruelly at you.

The inclination to preserve life is not necessarily bad—it is just so often misdirected. It urges us to forget that when we come to God, we relinquish every "right," that even my life is not my own. Precisely because this is so antithetical to my "human nature," I fear it. So I need God to help me overcome this lesser, unworthy fear.

If this does not happen, I will be enslaved by a fear of loss: loss of life, loss of comfort, loss of prestige—one fear or another will best me. But what if I submit to God and allow him to deal with my fear? Can he rid me of it? Yes. How? With fear.

The fear God promotes is healthy, sparked by an understanding of and encounter with the true nature of God. He is big, far larger than any other thing I will face. And he is awesome, far more powerful than any other force I might meet. And he is holy, far more pure than any other idea I could entertain.

So here's the question: Since my life will be affected by fear regardless of what I do, which fear will I embrace? A strange way to phrase it, perhaps, but accurate, since we are people subject to fear. Amos has a single answer: Fear God. When you hear the lion roar, don't run, don't ignore, don't even curl up and whimper. Let the fearsomeness of that sound focus you so that you can enter scary situations. These situations will most certainly come, but let's face it, once you've experienced skydiving, you will never again be bothered by a little turbulence on the commuter plane to Chicago.

It's a matter of degree. A lion's roar beats a high priest's mewling any day. This is why Amos can stare Amaziah down and win:

He has heard the lion, and everything else is just Muzak in the elevator. Threats bounce off this prophet, not because he's supremely self-confident but because he is so afraid.

Live in Fear

"Since, then, we know what it is to fear the Lord, we try to persuade men" (2 Cor. 5:11). This is Saul again, writing under his new name of Paul. Paul was struck blind after a voice from heaven (did a thunderous roar accompany the blinding light?) challenged his way of life. That was a life-changing experience for the former Pharisee; it affected every molecule of his being. From that point on he was dedicated to serving God. He had not been raised or schooled for this; in fact, his chosen profession was quite at odds with his new career move. But God took him and told him to go and preach. Paul did.

Paul was so changed by his exposure to God that everything about his life was affected. And he never quite got used to God. His awe for God—his fear of God—touched him deeply. Paul's evangelistic zeal was, as he makes plain in 2 Corinthians 5, the result of fearing God. As a result, churches started, lives changed, and a whole world was exposed to the good news of God's love.

The courage of Paul is legendary. He faced repeated trials and troubles, and he experienced great discomfort simply because he remained true to his Lord. But he never wavered. Like Amos, he stood his ground, not because he was arrogant or insane but because he was afraid.

"Live your lives as strangers here in reverent fear" (1 Peter 1:17). These are the words of Peter, a man who would have known Paul and experienced similar trials. Live in fear? Sounds like this guy has hold of what energized Amos. But wait. Remember Peter? He's the fellow who seemed very bold—"We'll die with you!" he promises Jesus. "Give me a sword and I'll lop off a head or an ear"—until he ran when a mere girl accused him of fraternizing with the enemy.

By the end of his life, his arrogance has evaporated along with his timidity. Live your lives in fear, he counsels. What happened?

What changed? Several things must have tempered Peter: repeated exposure to Jesus, especially after his resurrection, the sinking in of God's grace to him personally, hardship at the hands of countrymen bent on eradicating the Christian menace, a settling assessment that following Christ was in fact the only way to go. However it happened, we have this record of Peter's counsel to live in fear. Peter knew that roar as well.

Then there was Isaiah, who heard at the outset of his own ministry: "The LORD Almighty is the one you are to regard as holy, he is the one you are to fear, he is the one you are to dread" (Isa. 8:13). Holy, fear-inspiring—this is the picture of God for Isaiah, a man whose life is swallowed by the Lord. He hears God speaking, telling him the course to follow. Will Isaiah walk this road? Yes, but not all who hear the roar exercise the wisdom to do so.

Take Ananias, for example, a denizen of the early church who, with wife Sapphira, sold property and brought money to the apostles for distribution. Many were doing this sort of thing, and it was a viable way of assisting the needy. But Ananias and Sapphira had a scam: They would sell land, skim a portion of the proceeds for themselves, and still make a generous and widely heralded donation to the deacons' fund. Problem was, the game was uncovered, by Peter of all people. "You're lying about this, Ananias," said Peter. "No, I'm not," he protested. And then he died. Same thing happened later that afternoon with his wife. She is tested for veracity, fails, and dies. As a result, the text tells us, "great fear seized the whole church" (Acts 5:11).

This couple's fear of the future—their need to keep back something for themselves (Acts 5:2)—drove away the fear of God. Their subsequent deaths, however, instilled a "better" fear in those who heard the story, both those who were part of the church and those who watched from the wings (Acts 5:13). Why? Because of what was going on in that group. Or to be more accurate, *who* was going on. Because God is serious: He's real, big, and powerful.

When God gets loose in people, lives change. God takes them, changes them, sets them loose on adventures of their own. Like members of the early church, who lived steadily "in the fear of the Lord" (Acts 9:31), they never forget whom they serve; the sound of that roar always occupies space in their heads.

Courage on Display

In his eighth decade, Polycarp was hardly a physical threat to the vaunted Roman Empire. But this diminutive church leader, who in his youth had been a disciple of the apostle John, was a decided threat to the delicate weave of pantheism that knit the empire's disparate strands. So he, along with others of his ilk, was slated for death.

Word of this contract on him got out, and friends of Polycarp urged him to head for the hills. He shrugged off their concerns. Why would he consider abandoning God now? He moved to a nearby farm and kept about his business, until one day Roman soldiers came for him. He requested and received permission for a final session of prayer in his home. During that time, he prayed for everybody he had ever known, including his captors. It took hours. Then they left, so Polycarp could face the music.

The Roman governor seated in the Coliseum had an easy solution for the old man he was reluctant to have killed: A pinch of incense was all it would take, an over-the-shoulder, don't-really-mean-it indication of obeisance to the gods. Then we can all get back to normal, and you can go off to die of old age.

Polycarp smiled. "No dice," he said. "I haven't come this far with God to turn tail and run now."

"How about this?" the governor pleaded. "A public denunciation. A simple 'away with the infidels' to show us how you might feel about fellow followers of the Way."

Polycarp turned, gestured to the gathered crowd of bloodthirsty Romans seated in the bleachers: "Away with the infidels."

Something snapped in the governor. "Throw him to the lions!" But an official reminded the governor that could not happen this day. "Burn him!" he cried, and soldiers bundled the codger off to the pile of sticks and logs. They tried to nail him to the central pole. Christ will help me stand, said the old saint. So they tied him instead. The fire lit, they stood back to wait. But the flames formed an arch around Polycarp. Enraged, the soldiers ran him through with swords, and he died even as his blood extinguished the flames.

Polycarp died that day, a human sacrifice. One witness said he smelled like bread baking. A human sacrifice? Polycarp had been that for years, every day crawling up to the altar to die, the lion's roar ringing in his ears.

Just like Nate Saint. Together with four other pioneer missionaries, Saint moved to South America to take the gospel to people who had never heard it. How do you find such people, and when you do, how do you get their attention? Saint and crew used an airplane, with which they circled a remote jungle village and from which they dropped gifts. Finally, they landed, met some people, made friends. Or so they thought.

These people, part of the Auca tribe, were duplicitous. Known as headhunters and cannibals, they lived for the moment and did what suited them. They took the missionaries in for a time and then turned on them. One day, they attacked, running each man through with spears, all because of wounded pride. Five men died in a little river next to their little plane. They were strong men, athletes. One had a gun. They could have defended themselves from the attack they saw coming; one of the Auca warriors was perplexed that they did not retaliate in any way.

Their peace in the face of adversity made a profound impact. Many Aucas live today as citizens of God's kingdom precisely because these men "lived in reverent fear," refusing to give in to the simple fear of losing their lives or their way of life.[6]

The Transformation

It would have been far easier for Amos to walk or run away. He could have turned south for home, maybe done a little preaching along the way, and gone back to farming and grazing, cheered by having done so much of what God had asked. With simple acquiescence, he could have placated Amaziah and preserved his own reputation.

But Amos had cashed in his desire for self-satisfaction long before, the moment he had stood on that ragged path and seen the lion bound in front of him. A tame lion? Safe? Neither. Amos was flattened by the roar and never recovered. Like Paul. Polycarp. Nate.

Notice that the role of crusading preacher was custom-made—for Amaziah. Named by parents who wanted to say "the LORD is my strength," Amaziah had, as court priest, the prestige that would have ensured a hearing. Had he come with a word from God, people would have taken notice. But he denies his heritage and his God in favor of himself, leaning into a system of immediate recognition and gratification. Amos threatened that system and so had to be stopped.

But when you've met a lion and lived, you just don't get that worried about a mere priest who wants you to go home. Amos quickly dispatches Amaziah with a word of personal judgment and then delivers a final word of corporate condemnation, destined to fall on all who "trample the needy and do away with the poor" (8:4). God is about to unleash his fury on people who have been perpetually disobedient and devoid of fear. Amos describes a picture of destruction, when "the sinful kingdom" will be swept "from the face of the earth" (9:8) so as to eradicate completely its surface from "all the sinners" (9:10).

One might think after so long a diatribe that Amos would conclude his public efforts with this cacophony of judgment, but he does not. There is still the closing word from God, one of encouragement, mercy, and hope. With this, Amos is like the other prophets who can deliver the hard message and still cite God's goodness. Surprising perhaps, but consistent, since God's hope is for a turning toward him on the part of all.[7]

Some will not. Some hear the lion and move out of its path, find another road, and quickly forget their encounter. But others will be changed by the meeting. They let go of matters that might otherwise prompt the wrong sort of fear. They embrace what is good and true, despite the short-term price they most likely will pay.

For such people, the stormy "day of the Lord" closes with a glowing sunset over the beach, because they are reunited with the lion whose voice has helped to chart their course. They can anticipate life with him in rebuilt cities, among verdant crops, stable and rooted (9:14–15).

Fear the Lord. Don't be afraid. Blaise Pascal, a seventeenth-century mathematician who in his thirtieth year heard the lion roar, resolved the apparent paradox like this: "Fear not, provided you are afraid. But if you are not afraid, be fearful."[8] Fear, properly directed, is necessary. Fear is already innate; the real issue is whether we will capitulate to the destructive nature of this inherent fear or allow the more constructive fear of God to control it.

With Pascal, we can endorse fear of the sort Amos describes. When we meet the lion, we can rightfully shake in our boots and never lose that sense of awe, respect, fear. We should never minimize God to the point that we lose this sense; it should be retained so as to inform our decisions, our responses, and our actions.[9]

Amos demonstrated this uncommon sense when, after the roar, he went north to preach. Polycarp showed it with his resolute faithfulness in prayer. Nate Saint displayed it by circling the Amazon jungle in a plane, learning to communicate with cannibals, and dying peaceably.

And also with Pascal, we can courageously turn against people and situations that might otherwise provoke fear. It is this sort of fear that God wants to eradicate; the way he does this is by making us afraid—of him.[10] We need a direct confrontation with God to set us on a new road, where we are no longer chary of threats to personal well-being but choose rather to "work out . . . salvation with fear and trembling" (Phil. 2:12). That is, we walk the path God marks out all the while fearing the one who blazed the trail. Will we cave to pressure along the way? Will we capitulate to fear? No, not if we retain that roaring sound and maintain a healthy fear.

Amos is with Paul in this, as he is with John, Polycarp, Nate Saint, Pascal. These people and many more know about appropriate fear and do not give in to lesser distractions. Intriguing, that the boldest among the minor prophets should be the one to teach us the most about fear. But then, if what I am saying about fear is accurate, this is exactly right: True courage is rooted in fear.

Replace Fear with Courage

The Greek and Hebrew terms for "fear" convey a wide range of meaning. But the issue is not purely grammatical. There is a weightier, theological point, namely, that God is so big, so awesome, so terrible (from the Latin *terrere*, for "tremble") that he truly does strike genuine, unmitigated fear into the hearts of his people. But this fear does not, unlike the fear we often feel, debilitate. It means to clear the heart of distractions caused by the fear placed by sin so that life can proceed with courage and conviction.

As humans, fear is an unavoidable part of our nature, obstinate as obsidian and stubborn as boorish houseguests. It is there because initially God made us with the capacity—the need—to fear him. To love him, to enjoy him—yes, but also to fear him, recognizing that he is distinct from us, more awesome than us, worthy of our fear.

But in the same way the lunatic with a sledgehammer maimed Michelangelo's *Pieta* years ago, sin disfigures us. The result? Fear is still present, as resolute as marble, but it looks different now. It is marred and cracked and no longer functions as intended.

Now, fear is smaller, selfish, only as big as me or you. Originally fear was supposed to take us outside ourselves to recognize God, to make us stand back in awe and even terror. But fear has been hammered, and in the rubble lies a self that is easily threatened. We spend our lives trying to piece together the fragments; we are self-consumed. And when we loom so large in our own eyes, we are able to view God only as a nuisance or curio.

This is why God must come from outside to roar. We can no longer generate from within this proper fear; we must have it instilled by God. And when he roars, we have a choice to make. We can run to some place safe, to hide unperturbed. Or we can stand, rising above the heap of self to see Another. If we bolt, we risk distancing ourselves from the sound of God's voice. If we stay, there is an additional dilemma. Not only do we abandon fascination with self-absorption, but we actually put self to death altogether. It is a radical, demanding, serious choice we face.

Picture staying. Decide that a low view of God is unacceptable, that God really does have far greater worth than you can possibly imagine. Stand there before him or kneel or lay—and allow him to shake your self to its core. What remains of this core but a seed?

"I will plant Israel in their own land, never again to be uprooted," God tells Amos (9:15). The fig tender's final vision shows God as a farmer himself, taking seeds. He pushes them down into the dirt, suns them, soaks them. There are trees coming. They grow straight and strong, people tended by God who are full of courage because they are sunk deep into him.

God is the one who can "strike the tops of the pillars so that the thresholds shake" (9:1), which is why he deserves to be feared. Once we get this straight, we can approach him for help with the other matters that scare us. Perfect love drives away those fears, inviting us to replace them with a fear that develops in us courage for the life ahead.

7

STAY CLOSE
Hosea

You can stand your ground courageously, but when someone hurts you—when a person lies about you, walks away from you, disses you in public, lets you down, abuses your trust, steals your money or reputation, turns others against you—the natural inclination is to strike back or to leave. Both of these seem perfectly reasonable. Totally logical.

But both are wrong, at least in the realm bounded by God's parameters. In this realm, one "turns the other cheek"; one seeks to imitate Jesus, who "entrusted himself to him who judges justly" (1 Peter 2:23).

This makes so little sense. It is so much easier to get mad or get gone. Why not knock someone's block off? Why stay where the pain is, linger in a hurtful situation, head back into the lion's den, suck it up, let it roll off your back, grin and bear it?

If we have lived any time on this planet, spent any time in an office, classroom, warehouse, dormitory, church—if we have been around people—we know what it's like to get pounded. Sometimes we deserve dressing down. But often we're innocent or at least more innocent than the charges laid against us would infer.

Still, we get hurt. And with that experience come some natural reactions to hurt. They are not as godly as we'd like. We ought to respond with charity. Grace ought to well up inside and spill over. Compassion should be evident. But feelings war with spirits, and conflict occurs. We might stand and fight, sit and smolder, or pack up and leave town.

Or we might stay and love. That's what we'd like, in our hearts. We'd like for God to come in and sweep away the anger, the pain, the frustration so that we could see the person behind the latest barrage, with love. God could do that, couldn't he?

I have been embroiled in conflicts in which vinegar hit baking soda and caused a foaming mess. These were not surgical strikes, with a quick cut, speedy removal, and efficient stitches to ensure a negligible scar. Often the aftermath resembled the corner of our sofa cushion that was shredded by a frisky dog. Problems arose and persisted, ebbing and flowing, depending on a variety of circumstances. Sometimes, long after the supposed end had occurred, flares erupted.

In situations such as this, I recognize that God has a path for me to follow. It is not necessarily the road I would prefer—I would rather stuff the problem,[1] vent my frustrations in some spectacular manner, or just run away. What I notice is that I am not the first to face such dilemmas. I think of Hosea when I enter or am reminded of conflict. I wonder what it must have been like for him.

Hosea's story is regularly read as an allegory, depicting the relationship between God and his bride. The same thing happens with the Song of Solomon. There is something so achingly personal about both works that it seems almost intrusive to take them otherwise; we would not presume to pry open doors in the private lives of real people.

Allegory makes the personal content less intense, more applicable—and there is some virtue in this manner of interpretation, because both books do tell us something true about God. But what if they are also slices of real life? What if Solomon gives us a glimpse of the deep satisfactions, the rapturous joys, the sheer pleasures of a marriage relationship? And what if Hosea breaks silence about the agony of a wandering spouse? I would not want to miss the human message either: More marriages need wonder and passion; more spouses need wooing and permanence. More relationships deserve commitment.

People Who Do Not Stay

The "seeking" story is common, as a hero sets off on a quest—for the grail, adulthood, or some other elusive prize. The "staying" story—in which one remains at home or by the side of a lover or a friend—is equally powerful. J. R. R. Tolkien's Lord of the Rings trilogy combines both with Frodo, who sallies forth with a mysterious ring, and Sam, who stands by his side. Action draws us in, but the strong friendship keeps us reading. Sam's resolute loyalty to Frodo, whom he accompanies unswervingly into old age, infirmity, and to the brink of a final journey, never wavers. He is released in the end, and his loyalties shift—to wife and child, home and hearth. "I'm back," Sam says to them as the trilogy concludes. We are meant to know that, as always, he will stay.

We need to think more about staying. We are shifty people and restless: We change allies and interests often. It's something we have learned to do, to be. Noelle Oxenhandler explains that even for those gathered "under the same roof, it is more and more common for each to be tuned to a different medium: telephone, television, computer screen. If there is a music of family life, it is less and less like a rich and resonating chord than like a pattern of disparate melodic lines occasionally, randomly intersecting."[2] Connecting with others and staying with others is something few of us do. Even those who manage tend not to do so for long or well.

Loyalty is passé; "'til death do us part" has been exchanged for "as long as we can." Maybe we have planes, trains, and automobiles to blame, or media; maybe it's just our nature. Since Babel we haven't been very good at sticking together.

It's getting worse. Time was, people stayed put. You could go to towns and find many who had lived in one place all their lives. Now, that's historical, unusual. When we hear on the radio that "new house starts" are up for the fifth or tenth or twenty-eighth straight month, we realize that some person or family is moving into every one of those places. They are coming from somewhere—and it's usually not next door.

The "younger" generation has suddenly cottoned to the reality that they don't have to work for the same company for thirty years; tax and loan incentives in the city or a depressed county entice homebuyers and business owners to relocate; weekend travel specials create possibilities for Europe or the islands or the coast. I live and work among a community of people in which hopscotching across continents every two years is common; some of their kids have needed to have extra pages added to their passports. Is it any wonder we're not good at staying? We learn to move from an early age. Our worlds are huge, full of wide-open spaces. It takes little provocation to touch off that urge, so watch it, bub. You hassle me and I'm outta here.

This is what makes Hosea so compelling. He was beset by all manner of circumstance that would have made us scurry toward greener pastures: His God gave him a thankless job, his wife played the field, his kids bore steady witness to infidelity. But Hosea stays. Why?

An Example of Commitment

We meet Hosea as a prophet active "during the reigns of Uzziah, Jotham, Ahaz and Hezekiah" (1:1), kings of Judah. The opening of his book also mentions a king of Israel, Jeroboam. The implication is that Hosea's impact was long-lived and nationwide; despite the civil unrest between north and south, Hosea exerted influence in both Israel and Judah. The kings named are the same as those who appear in the records concerning Micah and Isaiah. Another implication: Something was afoot among God's people that was serious enough to warrant sending three prophets simultaneously.

The way these prophets convey God's message varies, however. Often it came through direct speech: Prophets spoke. Occasionally, it came through their lives, demonstrated by how they lived or what they experienced. This "parabolic" approach (see Hosea 12:10) was intended to make people pause and reflect.

Hosea's life forces thought. Some might have wished to dismiss or ignore him (Hosea 9:7), but the strangeness of his action, to say nothing of the tenacity of his love, invited scrutiny. What drove Hosea to do what he did? Is he simply a lonely, desperate man, or is there something we are supposed to see there?

"When the LORD began to speak through Hosea . . ." (1:2). Hosea was at the beginning of his public prophetic ministry.[3] Fresh to the task, he could ponder the august history of prophetic activity and find himself in awesome company. He could look ahead to a life with God full of seeing visions, hearing words, learning of God's intentions. He could know, too, that the prophet's lot is not always easy; there is often a cost involved with service of this sort.

Then, still at the outset of his public ministry, comes a direct, personal word: "Go, take to yourself an adulterous wife and children of unfaithfulness" (1:2). Adjectives routinely adorn a bride, but Hosea cannot be ready for the one God uses: His wife is to be "adulterous." It's a hard, harsh word, made to apply to the woman a young man would bring into his home. Not only is the choice of a spouse taken from him, but Hosea is meant to marry a whore.

We have to be startled by the word, by the sheer shock such an idea conveys. We need to be stunned by the inescapable fact that God calls the prophet to this on purpose: "because the land is guilty of the vilest adultery" (1:2). So there's a reason: God means for Hosea to live out in Judah and Israel what God is going through with his people; he uses the prophet parabolically. But it is still Hosea who gets the whore.

Something recoils in us at this. It's not *nice*; it's not neat. This will not teach easily in Sunday school next week, nor would it even be a topic for a women's tea or a men's prayer breakfast. Where *do* prostitutes as marriage partners fit in conversation?

Which is the point: We have to be gripped by the sheer incongruity, the vileness, the almost incredible inappropriateness of the situation so that we can begin to understand what Hosea experienced and demonstrated.

"So he married Gomer" (1:3). We hear no protest, smell no whiff of dissent, see no hesitation. A child is born, a son. More children will follow, but their parentage is less clear. Quite probably, they are "children of unfaithfulness," and Hosea must each day see their faces, along with that of his wife, and wonder about omniscience and divine benevolence.

There are long strings of text, as Hosea faithfully delivers the messages God has for people. These various words hover close to the theme of faithfulness and how the Jews have broken faith with God. Their own promiscuity arouses God's anger and prompts judgment from him (4:5–9). But he cannot get his people off his mind; he cannot abandon them altogether. "I am going to allure her," he says of his people. "I will . . . speak tenderly to her" (2:14).

The magnitude of such love is as startling as the ignominy of Hosea's union. Which also is the point: True love weighs. It does not set sail at the first sign of trouble but stays, steady and firm. A junior high principal made the point one day over lunch, as we were talking about the unruly nature of kids at his school. Their behavior shocked even some experienced teachers, and so this wise man stepped in to encourage them. "Here's what I think about saying to those kids," he said. "I can be nicer to you longer than you can be mean to me." That sounds, to me, like God.

The diptych of Hosea's personal life is completed in chapter 3. There, God instructs the prophet to "go, show your love to your wife again, though she is loved by another and is an adulteress" (3:1). Gomer has run off—again—and Hosea is sent to collect her. It's bad enough to have a wife of such character at home, but to search her out after her most recent indiscretions? Hosea goes. "I bought her for fifteen shekels of silver and about a homer and a lethek of barley" (3:2). These references elude us, aspects of a culture we do not know. In plainer words what happened is this: Gomer took off, sold herself, and was now on sale in the market, goods for the highest bidder.

For Hosea to buy her meant that he went out in public and paid—in public—for his wife. Why was she up on the block? Everyone knew, just as everyone would have watched Hosea—the prophet of God, no less—pay the high price and then collect his bride. Can you feel the humiliation in your gut?

"You are to live with me," Hosea tells Gomer, presumably when they have left the market and are once more back home with the kids. "And I will live with you" (3:3). Again, no resignation, no huffing and puffing. No yelling. No screaming at God for the terrible mess that is his life. "I will live with you."

There is radiating from Hosea this fantastic commitment to the relationship God has engineered on his behalf. Hosea did not choose this woman any more than he decided on his own to become a prophet. But called to both, he was faithful to each. We may want or value more freedom of choice with respect to spouse or career, but Hosea's example is undeniable: The commitment he demonstrates is the same God wants from each of his own. Once he is engaged in each of these relationships—with his wife and with his God—Hosea is completely dependable. He is dependent too, for only God can sustain the sort of life that hangs on like this.

The Staying Power of God's Love

Fast forward seven centuries, to a house in Damascus, a Roman city to the north of Israel. In this house sits another young man. He is praying; he is blind. A week ago, this fellow had the world at his feet: He was bright, respected, feared, powerful. Success followed him like a shadow, and he showed promise of even better days ahead.

His most recent exploits ended abruptly. He had set out on the latest in a series of crusades designed to eradicate a creeping threat to the status quo, and with the blessing of the establishment, carried documents that would have resulted in the imprisonment of many cultists. Saul was heading for Damascus to arrest, imprison, and oversee the death of Christians.

God had other ideas. On the road, God appeared and threw Saul, unceremoniously, to the ground. When the lightning flashing around him subsided, and the voice speaking to him stilled, Saul noticed he was blind. His traveling companions had to escort him to the city, where he wound up in the home of a man named Judas (Acts 9:1–11).

Saul had probably thought to capitalize on his training, experience, privilege, and pedigree; he had so much going for him! God directed his steps altogether differently. In Hosea's case, God took a righteous man and threw him into a morally suspect arrangement. For Saul, God took a corrupt man and made him a saint. For both, the results were similar: When you sign on with God, your life will change.

The change for Saul involved an immediate revocation of the privileged life. "I will show him how much he must suffer for my name," God promised (Acts 9:16). The rest of Saul's life—his name changes too, to Paul—is the story of that suffering, interrupted on occasion by brief periods of relative calm. Paul is called by God to a life of declaring the Word of God, and for his troubles he encounters mostly grief. But Paul is not daunted by reception to his ministry; he does not turn from obedience to the Lord. He is "lashed to the mast"[4] of gospel exposition, and he tells us why: "Christ's love compels me" (2 Cor. 5:14).

The love of Christ. Grammatically, the phrase covers two conditions: Christ's love for me, and mine for him. This love, expressed in both directions, is meant to form convictions and fuel service. It explains Paul and Hosea. It helps us understand Jesus himself.

"I have come," Jesus said, "to do the will of him who sent me" (John 6:38). He said this often, and it was said of him, both by contemporaries and by prophets.[5] The will of God involved work; the work required love; love engendered loyalty; loyalty meant he stuck around. "It is finished," Jesus proclaimed, assessing his work and the completion thereof. He did what he came to do. He offered this job performance review from the cross, on which he stayed. He could have come off the cross, or not gone to it, but he did, and did not. Love pinned him there—the love of God and the love for his people.

The love of Christ is inherently relational. It ties you to God and to people. It compels outlandish behavior such as taking the gospel to people who throw rocks at you, plot to kill you, or beat you with metal-tipped leather straps. This is the love that roots you in a home where your wife is loose, experienced in beds other than yours.

We blush; we turn away; we prefer to talk and think of something else. But we cannot, for love is too strong to dismiss lightly. When we who profess to be gripped by love and fools for love finally come to terms with Love, then we too will be willing to empty our hearts by pouring them into others, no matter what they do in return.

What did it mean for Hosea to love Gomer, to take her as his wife, to live with her? What does it mean for God to love us, to view us as his bride, to take up residence within us? Hardly a fair comparison, we muse. After all, few of us have practiced prostitution or any of a number of really terrible sins. The worst we've done is a little lying, a little anger, a little jealousy. Okay, a little idolatry too, a little greed.

But God loves us anyway. What to us seems no more significant than roadkill on the highway is to God as obvious as skywriting. And he loves us anyway. He does not shy away from us, does not waggle a finger of condemnation in our face, does not stomp off in exasperation. He loves, he comes, he stays.

God's love affair with his people is long-lasting: "Out of Egypt I called my son," he says (Hosea 11:1). Once again, as with Micah, the story of Egypt and the exodus appears to illustrate God's longstanding commitment to his own. They are insensitive to what he offers; they offer sacrifices to the Baals (11:2). They try to pull away; God loops them: "I led them with cords of human kindness, with ties of love" (11:4). They want to be rid of God (11:7); he cannot let go: "How can I give you up?" (11:8). He shows his hand over and again; he refuses to be guilty of giving up. True, he will punish rebellion (13:16), but his desire is for their repentance, for their allegiance.

In love you stake your claim; love nails your feet to the floor. So God stands, radiating his intentions. All it takes is acceptance: "Take words with you and return to the LORD. Say to him: 'Forgive all our sins and receive us'" (14:2). The result? Blessings (3:5; 14:6–7).

We Need a New Example

We are expert at leaving. We are tutored by cultures that prize dating, with its inevitable string of breakups. We avoid lifelong careers by taking temporary jobs in which we routinely evaluate perks, results, personal fulfillment. We change allegiances like clothes: If one store doesn't suit us, we'll go elsewhere; if one brand can be had cheaper than another, we're off. We are conditioned to expect the new, to want the new, to leave the old behind. I went shopping for a bike and saw one with a sale tag swinging from the handlebar. It looked good to me—shiny, unscratched—and the price was appealing. "Why the markdown?" I asked.

"Last year's model," the clerk said. "We wanna move 'em out."

"Anything wrong with it?" I queried.

"Nope. It's just old."

This tendency to leave is exacerbated by stress. Think of the person raised in an atmosphere of turmoil: One parent is entangled by substance abuse, the other is withdrawn or combative. Sparks fly often in this home, peace is largely absent, trust is missing completely, conflict is common. Time passes, and relational patterns imprint themselves on hearts. This person leaves home to begin life "outside": at college, in an office, with a church. When there is misunderstanding, as happens when people live, work, or worship together, what will be the likely response of this person? In youth, there was nowhere to go; with age, doors open, and conflict can be avoided. Quite possibly this person lives with packed suitcases, ready to be flung in the car trunk at the first whiff of difficulty. So conflict comes, a person bolts, and others scratch their heads in wonder, before life resumes, closing around a hole briefly left by the departure.

Change the scene a bit. Now you are the person around whom trouble swirls like river currents. As it pulls at you and pushes, what is going on in your heart? Do you look for others to blame, do you assume blame, or do you grow loudly angry or quietly frustrated? Do you stay and fight or run and hide?

One can leave by quitting the scene. One can leave by dismissing the relevant factors and steamrolling those involved. One can leave by withdrawing into silence: Your body is there but the rest of you is not engaged. One tends to leave.

We are not often taught or encouraged to stay. Poll a group of friends, a group at church. Ask, Do you enjoy conflict? The answer is obvious before the question is fully formed. Then ask, When something difficult enters your life—a health matter, a financial setback, a family problem—what do you tend to do, really? Again, the majority response—the honest answer from the heart—is that we tend to drift or run from the problem.

Why don't we stay? To some degree it is because of our training and our culture. But there's more, especially for those of us who must also factor in the presence of the Spirit in our lives. Could it be that we trust the Lord only when the sun shines?

Hosea, much like Job, Paul, or Jesus, demonstrates that life is rarely easy or linear; the twists and loops of normal existence are enough to make anyone dizzy. The dizziness makes us sick of the life that produces such discomfort, and we want to retreat, to leave. We seek out an equilibrium where we can walk a straight line unencumbered. We long for the quiet garden, and if we can find God there, so much the better.

Every life needs seasons of repose to be sure, and God himself incorporated such seasons—they are called Sabbaths and span various lengths of time—into the fabric of his creation. But Sabbaths presume work, and the work of life is to encounter others and incarnate Christ. When we set to the matter of "showing Jesus," what will happen? The kindness and grace that characterized him will shine through us. And more: The difficulties he encountered will be ours to face as well.

Paul spoke of "the fellowship of sharing in his sufferings" (Phil. 3:10) as though it were a normal part of life. Indeed, Paul claims to want this experience very much. We know of clubs that gather around shared interests, but to congregate—to fellowship—because of a mutual interest in suffering? Peculiar. Some might say masochistic, even, especially in the light of Peter's advice: "Rejoice that you participate in the sufferings of Christ" (1 Peter 4:13).

Should we go looking for trouble? Not at all. What these writers tell us, what their experience shows us, is that trouble comes. The real question concerns how we will handle it. There is no masochism here but grace to stand, and patience.[6] To face squarely a person in trouble or who is causing trouble is to show the face of Christ, because this is what he does.

And here we come back to Hosea once more and the way his story illustrates God's way. God is one who stays the course. His own people deserted him. True, they came back occasionally. They would stop in with gifts, or for a quick chat, or to drop off a request, or to mention a need, or to list demands. But faithfulness? Consistency? Love? Spotty at best.

In sharp contrast was the Lord. He remained faithful to people long accustomed to infidelity. The wonder is that he did not leave to search out others who might be more interested or to save himself the steady pain brought on by proximity. God stays.

When Love Stays

Shortly before the Second World War broke out, mission activity in Ethiopia was responsible for introducing the gospel to groups of previously unreached people. When the war came, the missionaries left, fretting about the spiritual condition of those who had recently converted. What would come of those who enthusiastically expressed interest in following Jesus? In 1945, missionaries rushed back to discover that in the south the church was flourishing. A few dozen believers in Soddo had grown to several thousand.[7]

The reason for this spectacular growth in the face of desiccating opposition was tenacity. Imprisoned, beaten, robbed, and killed for their faith, members of the Christian church in southern Ethiopia did not run away from their Lord or the people who mistreated them. In some cases, the persecutors were obvious: Government officials from both home and abroad did all they could to eradicate the church from the country. At other times, the difficulties were closer to home, as with Gifatei. She made life miserable for her evangelist husband, who took her to serve with him in another area where the gospel was needed:

> When he was hungry and tired and asked for coffee and food . . . I would mumble and grumble and take as long as possible to serve him. I determined I was going to make it hard for him, and I did. . . . I thought: it would be so nice to go back home. If I can only keep this up, he will soon tire of it all, and be glad to take me back home.
>
> Nearly every day I found some way of testing my husband. . . . But he was never upset with me. He would tell me about the different ones he had found throughout the day, how he had witnessed to them. He was happy when they had really shown an interest. . . . He seemed so encouraged and so happy. I was so upset and angry.

One day, Gifatei's husband brought home a man, the first person he had met who wanted to convert. He called Gifatei to celebrate with him.

> I thought to myself: Now look at that. Here I have to cook coffee for somebody else besides you? Am I going to have to tire myself out still more? Within me I was just so upset—and that is the way I felt all the time. . . . Finally the coffee was ready. My husband was happy, but not I. I did not have one bit of joy.

This day brought a breaking in Gifatei: The kindness of her husband and the conviction from God overwhelmed her to the point of confessing her bitterness and seeking forgiveness. In relating the story to friends, she asks:

> Pray for me, that I may be all the Lord wants me to be, and that I may make up for those days—those years—when I was so mean and so unkind, and did not realize the joy that could be mine in going out to serve the Lord.[8]

There was a change in this woman because there was no change in her husband. In the face of a storm churning the air of his home, he remained faithful.

A Message of Hope

God stays. God calls Hosea to stay too. Hosea does. He sets about the business of prophesying to an errant nation, all the while dealing with a turbulent home life. He marries a wife he knows will be trouble; he begins with her the semblance of normal family affairs, knowing they will be disrupted. He goes out searching and at great cost to his reputation and pride buys her back in a public, humiliating way. He does all this without complaint. When God speaks, Hosea obeys. When Gomer wanders, Hosea stays: steadfast, dependable, patient, and full of faith.

By opening the book on his own story, Hosea offers hope to those who face similar pain. I think of friends who have grown up in homes where divorce occurred. Their adult lives are marked by it; their relationships affected. A parent's divorce dampens one's own enthusiasm for marriage; the example of divorce establishes a pattern for dealing with conflict. When the child of divorce marries, will that person be likely to stay when the partner becomes unlovely?

I think of others who have been betrayed in relationships: People once considered friends turn on them with a sharpness that robs sleep, or they refuse their attempts to reconcile, or they misread their efforts to explain. Those betrayed—at what level is their energy for trying again? How motivated are they when it comes to making new friends?

Was it hard for Hosea? Are you kidding? We cannot sanitize these Bible folk to the point that they no longer resemble real people. Gomer's behavior must have left Hosea's heart in shreds. Moreover, God's insistence that Hosea seek her out and stay with her must have given him an anxious night or two more than once. What lingers in our minds and hearts, though, as we wind through this story, is the clarity of faith, hope, and love. Hosea trusts God to give good direction and to maintain his ability to obey. He holds out hope for Gomer's return and desire to remain.[9] And he loves. He stays where he is, engaged and alert, refusing to bail out, resisting the urge to lope off for greener pastures.

The other might leave; there is always that possibility. But that is not the responsibility we bear. For us who are part of relationships marred by trouble of different kinds, we are able to respond in a way that depends on and demonstrates the love of God. The calling for us is to go nowhere, but to stand, to stay. We bring to the relationship by the sheer force of our presence the love God intends to characterize dealings between and among humans.

It's hard. This is the hardest thing you will ever do: to stay while someone screams, "I hate you!" or to return to someone who says, "Leave," or to look for someone who ran from your love. To love fully and formatively is excrutiatingly difficult, because it forces you to face the fact that you cannot, will not, care like this on your own, and because it necessarily puts you in a place of pain.

But to love—to this, God's children are called. They are called to love, to enter the realm where the love of God surrounds them like sunshine, to radiate the love that restores withered souls. This love is not the product of will or desire but a gift from God, diffused to those who take him at his word. There is no other way relationships can survive the pressures imposed by society or personal experience. Unless relationships are infused with divine love, flowing to at least one of the people involved, they cannot hope to exist for long, and neither will they flourish.

For Hosea, as for Paul, Jesus, an Ethiopian husband—us— love is a matter of hammer and nails more than velcro, of in the room more than out the door, of here and now more than see you later. Trouble comes, up close and personal: This is a consequence of life rusted by sin. But God resides within his own, enlightens the realm they inhabit, even sanctifies the ground they occupy. So trouble need not control the situation nor evoke the wrong response. It is possible, when one is called, placed, and strengthened by God, to stand that ground. It is possible to stay.

8

KEEP YOUR HEART SOFT
Joel

A life sunk deep into God manifests behavior such as that of Hosea, who stayed close to a wanton woman. God's compassion was modeled by this prophet, and Gomer was one obvious beneficiary. What motivates behavior such as this? It's a matter of the heart: When one's heart is full of God, he cannot help but spill out.

Joel scrutinizes people who had become as hard and barren as high desert. He explains the problem in graphic detail, calls for a dramatic change of hearts, and describes what happens when God is again welcome in them. There is little else of concern in this book: We know virtually nothing about the prophet, nor are we certain about when or to whom he wrote.

The lack of chronological markers gives Joel a timelessness, just as the nonexistent biography[1] makes us focus on the message. It's just as well, because this book is a puzzler, and we need our wits about us to understand it. It skips easily from literal descriptions to metaphor and skitters across the time line in a rather disconcerting way.

Curses kick off the prophecy, as locusts scour the land, destroying its produce (1:4, 10). They seem an obvious fulfillment of Moses' predicted punishment for wandering from God (see Deut. 28:15–51). But there is wide discussion on the significance of Joel's opening lines. For example, these locusts that descend so suddenly: Are they real bugs or metaphors? A case could be made for either, and regularly is. The fact that Joel quickly shifts from locusts to an invading nation (1:6) tells us that for him the agent of destruction is secondary to the fact of destruction, its cause, and even its locale. What brought about this terrible situation? Disobedience—a refusal to be open to God. As a result, life was in disarray. Crops that should have been harvested were ravaged, gnawed to the root. Land that should have been verdant looked like *Macbeth*'s blasted heath. The priests were mourning, and joy was gone (1:9, 12).

Interesting comment, this last one, tacked on to a list that describes the withering of vines and trees. Why does Joel mention joy? One would not find this item in a book on horticulture; it is different in every way from a palm or a pomegranate. Indeed, it is this very difference that takes us to another "level" of meaning, for Joel's point about joy shows an interest not so much in landscaping as in interior design. He bemoans the terrible loss of pasture and produce, but he also wants us to go deeper. The countryside without plants serves as an image of hearts gone hard, devoid of God.

Hardened Hearts

Charles Dickens described the hard heart with his immortal Scrooge: "a squeezing, wrenching, grasping, scraping, clutching, covetous, old sinner! Hard and sharp as flint, from which no steel had ever struck out generous fire; secret, and self-contained, and solitary as an oyster. The cold within him froze his old features. . . . He carried his own low temperature always with him."[2] Scrooge later undergoes a miraculous transformation, aided by several "spirits," but we are first shown how closed he is. There are reasons, of course, as Dickens reveals during those "spiritual" encounters: Scrooge had a difficult father and developed early on a love for money. What captivates Dickens, and what gives this story such a biblical cast, is the emergence of joy. By the end of the *Carol,* Scrooge is singing a new song. The spiritual work has taken effect, and he is a happy man, full of joy.

Joy comes where God is at work, the result of taking pleasure in and drawing comfort from his connection and control. It emerges in people for whom God is real and significant and bubbles out in emotions ranging from profound satisfaction to outright giddiness. It has a present and a future connotation, which is why we can anticipate a coming time of lasting joy in God's presence, and we can enjoy right now relationships, the fat of the land, and the rest Sabbaths afford. All this results in a happiness, which George Müeller called "the first great and primary business to which I ought to attend every day."[3]

Müeller's days were remarkably full. By 1835, once he had established himself in Bristol, two thousand orphans were under his care. He remained there until he was seventy and then began traveling as an itinerant preacher. His enthusiasm spilled over on to Hudson Taylor, a protégé of sorts whom he supported financially. Müeller, like Taylor after him, grasped that the only way to manage life was to "rejoice in the Lord."

Joy should accompany God's presence among his people, which is why Joel is alarmed by its absence. If joy is not in evidence, God's presence and power are in short supply too. In God's absence, hearts grow dry and hard, unable to bear the fruit that pleases him.

What happened to cause these hearts to stray so far from God? There are several possibilities; hearts are notoriously complex. The machinations of the evil one, who is always opposed to the constructive work God desires, are at work. Our natures, too, are in opposition. So we miss appointments, shirk responsibilities, and make excuses about going where God is. We find ourselves growing uneasy; feelings of guilt creep in and linger. Passion cools, absence makes the heart wander, and the gulf widens. Other interests lure us and occupy our affections. We become like drunkards (Joel 1:5), addicted to what pleases us.

Or we become exasperated. The things we had hoped for, counted on, come to expect do not materialize. We are told to wait, to be patient, and we are, for a time. But time passes, and what we looked for does not come. Disappointment turns to disgust. Deferred hope makes the heart sick, as the Proverbs say. Our hearts get infected when what we want does not show.

There's confusion too, with developments around us. Why is *this* happening, we wonder, or *that*? This is Job's question, asked repeatedly. Surprisingly, only the following answer emerges: Some things happen because they fit with God's larger plan, and you may never see the whole of that plan as long as you live. That's an affront to those accustomed to having answers for nearly everything and for whom effect nearly always follows cause.

Idolatry is another factor, prevalent among the kings in whose courts prophets often roamed. These monarchs married poorly or made foolish alliances and took into their homes and land the gods of other nations. It happens. We give over the allegiance God deserves to lesser things and pay the price of a wasted heart.

Much of life moves us toward hardness against God, and there are days when we feel as though it's just no use: We will never progress. Doesn't nature teach us, we wonder in our quiet moments, that all things naturally decay? Yes. In fact, a dictum of science is the second law of thermodynamics. According to this "law," nature inevitably runs down, moves toward increasing decay, suffers entropy.

But entropy is inevitable only in a "closed" system, where nothing else enters and in which no new force is at work. Our natures are not closed systems: God is active in both physical and spiritual ways. He is capable of creating something out of nothing or transforming old into new. God steadily infuses this "system" with good, which means that progress is possible and not only decay.

Think of a heart as if it were a garden. If you leave it untended or ignore it for other pursuits, drought will dry the ground, and bugs will perforate brilliant roses or tassling sweet corn. But if you apply fertilizer and water (adding to the garden's "system"), you will promote growth; if you keep weeds at bay, you will encourage fruitfulness. If you prune and harvest at the right times, you will reap abundance. It's possible to have a wonderful garden, just as it's possible to have a joyful heart.

Come in from another angle, to deal with the matter of those confusing circumstances Job and many others faced and encounter still. It may help here to go to the symphony and listen. The music you hear, whether it pours from the National Philharmonic or the local middle school orchestra, how does it happen, and where is it going? When the musicians practice the piece on their own, no one of them knows the entire tune from the score set on the stand before them. But bring everyone together and seat them on a stage under the direction of a skilled conductor. When the baton falls, suddenly all the disparate tunes and snatches of notes make sense.

Music makes me wonder, Could God's method of operation be more art than science? What if God has composed an enormous symphony and is gradually and gracefully conducting it across cultures and continents and centuries—and if, from time to time, individuals catch glimpses of what he is up to and hear bits of a tune they can recognize, appreciate, or enjoy—but the whole of the piece is not yet finished? What if our "problem" is wanting to have the entire package on a disk we can play at will, insisting that it must make sense to us now. What if we lack the patience not simply for a season or even a lifetime but for the entire span between now and when God is ready to be done? Taken this way, heart problems arise whenever patience fails or when pride rises, demanding and belligerent. No wonder so many stray. No wonder the prophet must come and call us back into the chairs so we can play.

The Role of Priests

Joel does not work alone; he looks for help the priests might give in this enterprise. Often prophets are set against priests, targeting them as leaders who sway people from God, but here Joel enlists their aid. His instruction for them to don sackcloth and mourn and to call others to a time of fasting and wailing (1:13–14) anticipates a season of corporate repentance in which priests are in the vanguard.

This is the ground priests should have occupied, having been set apart since Aaron's day to model and encourage adherence to God's law. Their effectiveness ebbed and flowed over time. The sons of Eli, for example, acted reprehensibly, while Samuel led the nation with distinction. When the kings replaced judges, priests were subsumed by the royal court. They were co-opted as advisors or became leaders in idolatry. The prophets who denounced priests found ample reason for expressing God's disdain: An office he had initiated to help direct people to himself and his ways had degenerated badly.

Priests were meant to be captivated by God's will and way, to be freed from worldly concerns, cared for by the rest of the community and dedicated to service of God. They were to be holy and to stand as beacons of holiness for the larger community. The tragedy of priestly indifference to holiness never failed to arouse God's anger elsewhere, and given Joel's detailed charges against drunkards, farmers, and vintners, it is likely the prophet would have condemned priestly shortcomings in his day had they existed. The fact that he notices instead their "mourning" (1:9) suggests that these religious leaders were potential allies of the prophet's cause and valued for their contribution of intercession (2:17).

The Reformation has influenced the contemporary view of priests. On the one hand, by emphasizing "the priesthood of all believers," its thinkers rightly illuminated clerical excess and lay reticence. On the other, Reformation thinking also laid groundwork for a devaluing of those called to and skilled for priestly ministry. Too often the "priests" of our congregations are now expected to function more as corporate executives than as spiritual shepherds. We do well to recover a healthy attitude toward priests—or whatever name they're given in particular faith communities—freeing them for devotion to study, prayer, and interaction with those communities.

Priests act as guides for river rafters, able to help because they spend so much time on the water. When others come to shoot the rapids, these guides do not say, "Wait here, and we'll tell you what it's like." Rather, they ride along, ready to assist, to point out features otherwise missed, to prepare those in the boat for what lies around the next bend.

Priests function as seasoned professors, trained for and skilled at rooting students in history and fashioning wings so that they can fly farther afield. The professor is not merely a machine spitting data but a compassionate person who interacts with students. Lives weave together far past ivied walls and gilded diplomas.

Priests are necessary. We cannot think their contribution incidental or easily made by others in their spare time. Nor should we burden priests with so much else that focus blurs. We learn this from Joel's directions to the priests near him: Their assistance is beneficial, but they should have perceived people's problems sooner.

Hearts Freely Opened

Joel can use the help. He sees judgment coming, as certain as a powerful army's forward progress. This inevitable "day of the LORD"[4] (2:1) includes a reckoning, when all are required to give an accounting of their words and deeds. It is a hard message, and it prompts a series of prophetic warnings—cast as previews, really—that are meant to awaken hearts. God prefers that people enjoy life more than fear judgment, and so he sends his prophet to rouse the rebellious.

This coming day is dreadful, and the prophet wonders who will be able to endure it (2:11). His question is rhetorical, for there will be some who can. They are those the psalmist identifies, who walk blamelessly, practice righteousness, speak truth, love neighbors, shun evil, honor the Lord, deal honestly, and lend freely (Psalm 15). Their lives withstand judgment because they have hearts fixed on the Lord.

So many hearts are not. So many hearts are closed off to God, full with concerns other than those of God. Occupied hearts such as these hang "no vacancy" signs and bar their doors. God could come to these preoccupied hearts with forceful insistence. He could barrel in and break through any resistance. He does not. He stands, like the eager suitor, and knocks to request entrance. He knows that only hearts opened freely will be able to bear fruit.

The wonder is that he wants hearts like ours. We who range so far from him, who fashion excuses as to why we must be gone, who put our hope in what does not last, and who depend on what cannot satisfy to meet longings we can barely contain: He wants *our* hearts. "Return to me," he says, "with all your heart" (2:12). Not much to bring, this heart. We had hoped for a springtime romance when we set our hearts on pursuing what we loved. What we got was winter's freeze, and our hearts turned cold and hard.

Which is why they must break. "Rend your heart," he says next (2:13). Not, move a little closer, do a little better, carve out a little space for me. Rather, shred this sacred place in your life that until now has been given over to other lovers. Furrows must be torn into the garden plot so that seed will grow, just as clothes were torn to indicate a person's sorrow and intention to be newly available to God's planting. The same is true for a heart in which God's fruit can begin to flourish: It must be shredded first to admit that seed. The "rending" of a heart differs from the locust-like stripping of a heart in that it prepares the way for constructive developments rather than being the result of dissipation.

God's Work in Human Hearts

The prophet calls us back. And what if we listen? What if the drifter reappears, if the rebel returns? A story Jesus told—the tale of the Prodigal Son—illustrates that very situation. The boy leaves a privileged position to forge his own way but wastes his resources on profligate living. Destitute, he finally slinks home, counting only on his father's reputation as an employer. What he discovers instead is his father's prodigal grace, spent lavishly even on fools. The son is welcomed back a hero, and there is no recriminating word, no condescending stare, no record book imperiously opened to show how far short he has fallen. Instead, the father hauls out a splendid coat and makes plans for a feast.

It's the surprise ending to a story we thought we had already figured out.

God's promise to pay for our problems dazzles. People brought
trouble on themselves by virtue of their own vices, and as we are
often quick to say, they should have been prepared to suffer the
consequences of their actions. That mechanism is upheld often
in Scripture, but not always; the best exception of course is God's
gracious provision of salvation. The consequence of sin is death,
as Scripture affirms repeatedly, but the impact of God's love is
life. He is even willing to absorb the cost of the consequences in
our lives.

More than willing: God comes, calls, invites. And some, tired
of the running, the pushing, the scrabbling on their own, respond.
We know we've made a mess of things. We want our lives restored.
When God does this, when he takes us in and cleans us off, we're
elated. Then, for some at least, a sense of shame wells up within.
I did this, to you? we think. We cannot bear the thought of our
rebellion and its effect on God. Amazingly, he takes the shame
and puts it away. He refuses to hold us accountable for the wickedness we chose to perform.

He could hold that over us, demand that we feel the pain of
our own impropriety. But the Lord will not grind us down into
the dirt of our rebellion as a way of making us pay. True, we are
likely to experience the effects of our wanderings; the Prodigal
still smelled of pig even after he was robed by a fine garment. But
God disarms our shame by filling us with joy.

It is the same for Joel. The devastation brought on by those
locusts was simply too great to be undone by human hands.
Only God can bring rains that will renew barren soil, only God
can restore life for crops sheared to the root, only God can cover
the shamed, only God can redeem time that was carelessly killed.
He is a God who burns the records of insurrection and dips into
his own resources to replenish accounts depleted by rebellion.
Because he intends for people to be confident and to live abun-
dantly, it follows that he will step in to help often and generously. Sometimes this help is material; always it has a spiritual
dimension.

God wants to be gracious (2:13). We who are familiar with deals and sales and come-ons find this nearly impossible to believe. God longs to be gracious. We who are so quick to manipulate others or send them packing on guilt trips can hardly fathom such desire. The God who calls for repentance quickly grants forgiveness? The beauty of this effect is not linked with any discernible cause; it is more art than science.

The Poured-Out Spirit

We call this beauty "grace," but we must take care that familiarity with the term does not rob its power. God's grace is more than an expression of "unmerited favor," as the prophets make plain. Yes, God does forgive, but notice what he forgives: the willful acts of proud rebels. These are not babes crying for a new diaper or bottle, whose parent comes despite the child having done nothing to deserve it. They are rather those who shook their fists at God, turned their backs on him, or gave themselves to imposters or competitors. Their hearts were corrupt and their attitudes hard. They were scheming anarchists, rebels, murderers. It was to such people that God showed kindness: thinking, aware, hard people. For mercy to flow instead of destruction, or even withdrawal, is amazing indeed. Grace is the kind expression of mercy from a God who has been terribly wronged.

So when God extends blessing to those who rend their hearts and make room once more for him, he is doing something wonderful and awesome and completely beyond human comprehension. We can hardly imagine the extent of his kindness, for he says through the prophet that not only will he make once ruined ground fertile again, but he will even pay for the damage done previously (2:25).

How do we manage a God like this—what categories can we find for grace of this magnitude? Then, just when we begin to find a handle or two, he gets bigger: "I will pour out my Spirit on all," he promises (2:28). This is the crowning blessing, the one that follows after all others (2:28). It is still future for Joel but no less certain, and the promise is meant to convey widely God's pleasure with and acceptance of those who have returned.

We know that this "pouring" of Spirit occurred at a first-century Pentecost when Peter and other disciples spilled into Jerusalem's streets with a profusion of "tongues." But as we examine this Pentecostal experience, we argue about it, disagree as to its implications and relevance; we wonder whether what happened then is meant to happen now or never again. And we miss—the Spirit.

Prior to Joel, the Spirit was known incidentally and occasionally, coming to specific people for brief bursts of activity. There were hints about a wider distribution; a few prophets anticipated broader spiritual influence. But for the most part, Spirit was a distant hope at best. Joel shatters this with his bold proclamation of the Spirit's coming, regardless of age or gender. He must speak loudly, for so many have hearts that dampen hearing. If you're living in his era, you can hardly believe your ears.

Has the situation changed? Can we sense the Spirit better now, with the benefit of two millennia's passing? Current discussions of Acts 2 would often suggest not; more energy gets expended on the what than the why of Spirit-pouring. So ask yourself, Why did Peter interpret what happened that Pentecost day in Jerusalem in terms of Joel's prophecy? We should ask this because the modern discussion so often hinges on an understanding of those "tongues," even though Joel never mentions tongues. What was Joel seeing that Peter later saw?

This: that God intended to seed furrowed hearts and to water them with his poured-out Spirit so that hearts would blossom and bear good fruit. The Spirit would come with power for the people of God, empowering them to live for his glory. This happens with obedience, which keeps the curses at bay.

With Spirit in their lives, God's people are marked as his own (see Eph. 1:13 for this language). It is a spiritual mark more than a physical one, acting in much the same way as a brand on a horse identifies its owner. Peter, on Pentecost, stands at the point of the fulfillment of the plan God had announced centuries earlier. "Tongues" are just one result of the Spirit's arrival; what we are meant to notice is that the Spirit has come on people who are soft and open to the Lord.

Joel's original prediction falls over those who are on the brink of coming back to God after a long, rebellious absence. It is to these people that the promise of the Spirit comes—people who have arrogantly abandoned God in favor of other pursuits and yet who are targets and recipients of his grace. The fact that God would be willing not only to receive back the sinners but also to mark them indelibly as his own is absolutely beyond comprehension. Perhaps this is why Peter speaks with such certainty and forcefulness, why that apostle's listeners are "cut to the heart" (Acts 2:37).

Hearts That Belong to God

The heart, as any physician can tell you, is where life resides. Hearts need exercise, a good diet, and low stress to perform properly. Some hearts are strong; some have holes. Some need patching or replacing; others pump without a hitch. You have a heart for as long as you live, be it ninety years or ninety minutes.

The heart, as any salesperson can tell you, is where emotions reside. The "heart" symbol, bright red and symmetrical, instantly conveys this understanding. Birthday cakes, balloons, and greeting cards come in the shape of a heart, in order to send the simple message, I love you.

The heart, as any pastor can tell you, is where faith resides as well. Do you believe that with all your heart? a pastor wants to know. In some circles, they write down when a person asked Jesus into his or her heart.

When God speaks about his interest in human hearts, whether through Moses, the psalmists, Paul, or Joel, he is dealing with this juxtaposition of physical, emotional, and spiritual concerns. Your heart, he asks, where is it? With what are you filling your heart; toward what are you aiming it? As his revealed Word indicates over and again, the Lord wants pure hearts, undivided hearts, sincere hearts that are occupied fully with him. He is after those who love him, serve him, enjoy him wholeheartedly.

Joel comes because hearts are far from God. The prophet speaks in the most dramatic way, culling from the corporate memory images of locusts and armies that depict ruin and despair. For Joel the heart is like a rolling plain stretched out to the horizon, open to possibilities. The green grass, the flowering trees, the neat rows of vegetables on this plain all speak of promise, potential—a wildness, too, as is always the case with growing things. Weeds jostle for position, eager to occupy space tomatoes and oaks want; bugs do more than provide a sound track for this vibrant picture. Destructive, marauding forces lurk on the edge of our hearts too, and Joel tells us what happens when they gain access.

The prophet's news: This powerful opposition can be checked. No force is greater than God, and so he can triumph even over the locust swarm or the apparently invincible army. We affirm this theologically, and we know it practically too, from the stories we hear. People whose wanderings took them far from God tell how when they turned toward him and saw what he offered, they were stunned, then grateful, then shocked, then devout. Their experience gives me hope about others still out there, and I hear in Joel more about possibility than condemnation. The prophet's warnings are not the gloatings of a deity about to pound his errant subjects but the cries of a wounded lover who longs for reunion with his beloved. "Come back," he says. "Open your heart."

Hearts, like gardens, need cultivating. If you neglect either, even briefly, the wilderness moves in. So instead of flirting with disaster, we must focus on the Lord. We must admit to hearts that are easily distracted and seek his help. Then we can enjoy his abounding love and compassion (Joel 2:13) by coming often into his presence, by thinking frequently about his character and provision, serving gladly in his kingdom, welcoming his Spirit, and taking pleasure in being marked and known and empowered by the Spirit.

In "Thou Hast Made Me," John Donne, the seventeenth-century poet and priest, puts it like this:

> Thou hast made me, and shall Thy work decay?
> Repair me now, for mine end doth haste.
> I run to death, and death meets me as fast,
> And all my pleasures are like yesterday.
> I dare not move my dim eyes any way,

Despair behind, and death before doth cast
Such terror, and my feebled flesh doth waste
By sin it, which t'wards hell doth weigh.
Only Thou'rt above, and when towards Thee
By Thy leave I can look, I rise again:
But our old foe so tempteth me
That not one hour my self can sustain;
Thy grace may wing me to prevent his art,
And Thou, like adamant, draw mine iron heart.[5]

How can a heart be ready for God's plants to grow there? Follow the course this prophet charts: repent, return, receive. Resist any call away from God that entices you to see anything other than God as worthwhile. Listen to his clear voice, cling to him as your refuge, depend on him for protection (3:16).

Joel's prophetic ministry ends with his barren desert becoming a teeming rain forest, where the mountains "drip new wine" and the hills "flow with milk" (3:18). A transformation is unmistakable, on both the physical and the spiritual level. What changed? God's invitation went out; human repentance took place; the promised Spirit arrived and took up residence in hearts. With a full pardon (3:21), even guilt is banished, so there is plenty of space for good things to grow.

Like holiness and happiness. Plants such as these flourish in well-watered soil where weeds and bugs are quickly removed. In cultivated hearts that "set apart Christ as Lord" (1 Peter 3:15) and purpose to trust and obey him, beauty and good fruit are abundant. This happens because such hearts are receptive to the poured-out Spirit.

Prophets and priests alike helped prepare people for the day when God would dwell among them. Some thought of this in distinctly physical terms, but in light of the teaching of Jesus and the apostles, we know God planned to be more personal. According to them, God's Spirit is capable of permeation and of establishing residence in a space as small as a human heart. This is what he desires, the intensity and intimacy of personal space. Hearts open to his ways are open to him so that he can come and live there. "The LORD dwells in Zion!" (Joel 3:21).

$\overline{9}$

RADIATE INTEGRITY
Malachi

The priests Malachi knew were different from the devout, mourning intercessors Joel addressed. Malachi's priests were sneaky; their hearts were divided. So this prophet blares like a foghorn in the mist, sounding a series of short, intense blasts against the imminent danger of hypocrisy.

Malachi spoke to a post-exilic people, whose story we know in part from reading Ezra and Nehemiah. Most Jews had been in Babylon during the seventy-year exile, until, with the encouragement of Persia's ruler Cyrus and under the inspired leadership of Joshua the high priest, Zerubbabel the godly governor, and the two prophets Haggai and Zechariah, they returned to their Promised Land. There they rebuilt the temple leveled by marauding armies. It was an act of reverence, reversing the exile-inducing indolence their forebears had shown toward God.

Sixty years passed, and Darius, Persia's new ruler, sent Nehemiah to Israel as governor. Under Nehemiah's indefatigable leadership, Jerusalem became once more a city of standing, a city with walls. Though the land enjoyed little of its earlier political prowess or prominence, its inhabitants settled in to a life of uneasy peace in the shadow of other powers. During this time, they reaffirmed their covenant with God. Part of this rededication involved the hard work of difficult and necessary change: Marriages with foreigners were dissolved, finances were redistributed, and leadership responsibilities were reassigned. Sabbath rest was enforced. Temple service began again too, and with it animal sacrifice resumed.

But the priests were a persistent problem. In the absence of Jewish kings and with the installation of foreign-appointed politicians, it fell to the priests to provide spiritual and moral guidance for the nation. Some, like Ezra, set a godly example. But many others, such as Eliashib (see Neh. 13:4–9), seemed interested only in personal prosperity. You would think that the exile would have taught an unforgettable lesson about fealty to God. As the record shows, it did not.

Malachi detects among the priests a pervasive attitude of playing at the things of God rather than being shaped by and submissive to them. This cast aspersion on God and eroded their trustworthiness in public. It also meant that as individuals these priests were increasingly hollowed out by the lack of coherence between what they should have done and didn't, by what they professed to believe but did not accept.

The Beginning of Hypocrisy

Hypocrisy starts small. Often it gets a foot in the door with minor inconsistencies, matters that are tiny enough to escape notice. For these priests, hypocrisy began with the sacrifices. "You place defiled food on my altar," God says. "You bring blind animals for sacrifice" (Mal. 1:7–8). These actions demonstrate contempt for God's name (1:6), but they easily escape the attention of others. The priests can still go through the motions of sacrificing, can still lead animals to the sacred place, slaughter them, and burn their bodies in accord with the law, but the meat they offer there is tainted, as God knows.

The priests know this too, but the people do not. To them, appearances are kept, and the priests come out ahead: They have saved money by buying previously offered food; they have exchanged sick animals for whole. And only God knows.

Small things matter. This was stressed in a writing course I taught at a local university. The students exhibited interest in the broad sweep of ideas, stories, and descriptions but had little energy for spelling and grammar. Despite their protests, we labored over those details so that their writing would not lose its impact.

Details count. Coffee mugs, posters, and bumper stickers disagree. Don't sweat the small stuff, they counsel. And it's all small stuff, they add. But such advice is wrong on both counts. Each of the little things—the quick comments, rapid thoughts, attitudinal shifts, instant decisions—each of them has weight, consequence. Each reflects and contributes to the shaping of character.

We might be inclined to argue, based on this passage from Malachi, for excellence in all we do, especially as it relates to God. The priests brought gimpy animals, we could say. Let's make sure ours are perfect. But the force of this passage does not lie with the relative skill with which we perform our duties or even with the quality of what we bring to the task. It lies, rather, with our sincerity. Do the concerns of our hearts, the words of our mouths, and the acts of our lives match up? Is all our talk of God just words?

Holding God's Name Lightly

In our day, God is referred to widely. So Joan Osborne croons, "What if God was one of us?" In *Life after God,* Douglas Coupland writes about "children of the children of the pioneers" who, as the first generation raised without religion, are desperately trying to negotiate the vagaries of life without the benefit of God. The disappearance of God leaves Coupland's protagonist Scout wondering, "We have religious impulses—we must," insists Scout.

"And yet into what cracks do these impulses flow in a world without religion? It is something I think about every day. Sometimes I think it is the only thing I should be thinking about."[1]

God shows up outside art too. The American Association for the Advancement of Science sponsored the "Cosmic Questions" symposium near Washington, D.C., in April 1999. It featured a debate between Steven Weinberg and John Polkinghorne. Weinberg shared the Nobel prize in 1979 for discoveries connected with unified field theory; Polkinghorne, now an Anglican priest, distinguished himself in the study of particle physics and is a Fellow of Britain's Royal Society. Their topic? The significance of God in the universe.

To speak of God anymore takes little provocation and garners little censure. The really interesting question, though, deals not with the existence of God but his significance. On a plane in southern Chile, I fell into conversation with a mathematician who had come from Spain to be part of a conference in Latin America. After he learned that I was a pastor, we started talking about God. Turns out this Spanish mathematician was struck by the beauty inherent to mathematics, a beauty that he—along with many of his colleagues around the world, he assured me—was inclined to attribute to some "exterior force." "Some call this God," he confided, "but for me? I find the idea of God neither contradictory nor necessary."

This candid conclusion sounds remarkably similar to what Malachi must have heard in his day among people who flicked back and forth between God and idols like shuttlecocks. What made Malachi's situation more grievous was the indifference he detected in priests who should have known better and more.

Malachi wades in among people whose awareness of God is keen. Their allegiance to God as a relevant, shaping force for personal life, however, is minimal. A hundred years of relative peace and prosperity have dulled their sensitivity, and the earlier patterns of neglecting God have started to reemerge. Once more the people risk the consequences of life without God. They have grown fat and happy; their temple has been built, the walls are intact, crops are growing, production is up, and turbulence is down. In the bright warm sun of prosperity, relative safety, and unbroken routine, memory fades like upholstery. People forget God. They still go through the motions of obeisance, but their hearts are not engaged. This is life after God, in which God is more concept than person, more sand than fire. People who once held him in awe now imagine that he can be easily placated and dismissed.

These people needed to recover honor for God and reverence. "I am a great king," God insists, "and my name is to be feared among the nations" (1:14). To revere is to be awed in fresh ways,[2] to peer with a jeweler's scrutiny at this precious God and walk away breathless. Malachi knew how often so many were prone to scoot by without looking, commuters on a train steaming through fall colors with their noses in a book. He brings the Word of the Lord to people who have lost the wonder of God. They see no luster in being God's chosen, find little moment in the sacrifices, give new meanings to obvious concepts, hold back what is not theirs to retain, find it futile to render obedience. The Persians rule, the king is dead, life goes on. How real is God?

Routine has replaced reverence. In the name of God, the sacrifices are made, but this name makes little difference as to the type of sacrifice or the heart it is meant to reflect. God's name has become contemptible and common. The passion of relationship with this God has given way to plodding through a set of rules. Sacrifices are made, lessons given, service rendered, offerings brought—all by people who hold God's name lightly.

"You shall not misuse the name of the LORD your God" (Exod. 20:7). So wrote the Lord, in stone, on tablets Moses lugged up Sinai. As one of the foundational Ten Commandments, this sits at the core of the Jewish legal system. By extension, it also applies to followers of God today.

For some of us, it was taught as a proscription against cursing, swearing, or "blaspheming." It covered the waterfront: "God," "Jesus," "Christ"—used singly or in combination—were neither to fall from lips in anger nor to be trivialized by idle talk or doodling. That's a good start; the name of God is different from other names and deserves special attention.[3]

Look again. The verb that translates "to take" is used more often to describe "carrying" than "using." This suggests that the Lord is referring to an attitude among those who "take" his name—those who are called into and agree to join his family, people who walk in and depend on the name of the Lord (for some backup data, see Micah 4:5; Zeph. 3:9; Zech. 10:12; 13:9). The word carries a warning: Do not enter this relationship lightly; do not trivialize your connection with God; do not suppose that having given assent you may now proceed with life as you please; do not let this decision be of little worth to you. Something should come of your bearing this name; do not take it upon yourself in vain.

Jesus embedded similar urgency in the model prayer he taught his disciples. "Hallowed be your name" was the phrase, as familiar to us as the Ten Commandments and just as likely to be undervalued. To "hallow" the name of God means to make that name holy by means of a life that reflects well on the nature of God. I cannot hallow his name if I claim to carry his name but live opposed to him. I make the name holy as my life radiates my lofty opinion of God, as I act out of love for him.[4] To claim allegiance and then to act insubordinately is to manifest the hypocrisy that God abhors.

Joel looked to the priests to provide warning about such misbehavior. When people strayed so far from God, Joel sought the priests for help with intercession. Through Malachi, the Lord continues speaking to priests, explaining that their lips "ought to preserve knowledge" and from their mouths people "should seek instruction" (2:7). They are meant to be, according to God, guardians and beacons, precisely because of these tendencies toward hypocrisy.

Priests appeal to tradition and point to the horizon; they skate on the two blades of stability and creativity, and they maintain a balance. It is not enough to esteem only the past or the status quo. Nor is it sufficient to crave only what is relevant and cutting edge. The former, devoid of the future's energy, will rot. The latter, loosed from any historical benefit, will have the impact and longevity of disco music.

Prophets stood outside the community, holding a magnifying glass. At times they would peer in, examining lives and noticing flaws. On other occasions, they focused light and started fires. Priests were different. They were embedded in the community and interdependent with it. They counted on others for land and sustenance; they contributed by preserving knowledge and making instruction available. When they failed, others suffered. Their lack of integrity contributed to the community's disintegration.

Shading the Truth

Another pothole on the priests' road was a tendency to shade the truth. This is understandable, since so frequently a small lie, a slight coloring, the tiniest adumbration would really help matters. Is it really so bad to hold something back, to shift the emphasis, or to fill a gap? Especially when it would improve standing, deflect blame, or add pleasure? We become masters at "spinning" the truth and then develop the ability to justify thoughts and actions. We might start with a desire for truth, but once we're out for a drive, we find that it needs some tweaking in order to maneuver the hairpin turns life so often takes. It isn't long before expedience grabs the steering wheel and slings truth into the backseat.

I was supposed to clean rooms before leaving the residence hall for a college break. It wasn't a hard or even a time-consuming job. But I was in a rush, and so I did a less than thorough job. A couple weeks later, the director in charge of that dormitory floor called. "This was your job," he reminded me. "You said you would; you said you did." I had not followed through, and he had found me out. I stood before a man I respected, head down in shame, caught. I had rationalized my behavior at the time but now realized I was wrong.

I keep doing this too. The shades, the spins, the lies—they ripple the silver of the mirror that reflects my heart. It's not a pretty picture. The solution? A rigorous commitment to truth, to correcting misstatements, to meaning what I say, to standing by what I have said. I challenge my kids on this, as any good parent should, but always the finger I point leaves three more aimed at me. Will I hold to the truth?

John spoke to friends, "children walking in the truth" (2 John 4), and to Gaius, who was on the same path (3 John 4). It's a lovely picture, these saints who roam the way of truth, and it serves as a marker: This is what I want to crave as well. For Jesus, truth was essential. "I tell you the truth," he said on numerous occasions. He could be trusted, in other words. His words might not have been easy to swallow, his argument not all that attractive to people determined to be free moral agents, but his ways were honest and forthright. He stood for, trumpeted, the truth.

"Sanctify them by the truth; your word is truth." Jesus again, quoted by John (17:17). Jesus is praying for his followers, because he knows they will have a tendency to drift from the truth. They will be captivated by other possibilities. They will weasle out of responsibilities, shift the focus, throw off the blame, refuse to live according to standards that God established.

Your Word is truth. The people God addressed through Malachi did not buy this. "All who do evil are good in the eyes of the LORD," they insisted (Mal. 2:17). It's a perversion, this reasoning, a handy way of rewriting the Word of the Lord. It sounds like something out of Orwell's 1984, in which the politicians were expert at "doublespeak," according meaning to words that was contrary to how they had long been understood.

It is not as though God deliberately hides his intentions. His way—his Word—is quite plain. Demanding, to be sure, but plain. It is we who twist things for our own benefit, fitting God to personal preference or experience. I once challenged a young man about relationships and showed him several relevant passages of Scripture. He looked at them, looked at me, and declared, "It doesn't say that." I balked. Could he not read? He could, of course; he was an intelligent guy. But his heart had written a lexicon of convenience such that words meant what they needed to mean in the context of his own desires.

You see the tension. The alternative requires accepting a standard that has demands that are not always, well, appealing. So what standards will I accept? What will be the basis for my decision?

This brings us back to God. If I accept that God exists, then I must go a step further to ask, So what? It is simply not enough for God to have a dispassionate existence unconnected to human life; what manner of god is a god such as that? But if I accept that God's existence has implications for my life, then logically I will have to explore the nature of those implications. Or I will have to fashion strategies for living with cognitive dissonance, distancing myself from this logical stream and drinking at other brooks.

Loving Money

Hypocrisy is not limited to priests; anyone can succeed at it. After promising a refining of the Levites (3:3), Malachi broadens his invective to include all who are withholding "tithes and offerings" (3:8). It is a charge that sends us to our own checkbook. What does its ledger say about me? About my faith? One of the biggest problems with wealth is that it insulates us from God; when we have enough money, our need for faith diminishes. Of course, there is a debate about what constitutes "enough," but the idea is plain: Money gets in God's way.

Malachi's third chapter often shows up in a sermon series on "giving," or when a church is preparing for, in the middle of, or stalled during a capital fund drive. "Tithe!" the speaker enjoins, explaining how that old-fashioned term means 10 percent (of gross or net is a point of quibbling). "Tithe! And see if you don't notice results. Remember—this command comes with a promise!"

True enough. But when we punt to this passage only when funds are low or nail it as a plank in our boardwalk of rules, we miss something. What prompts the Lord to raise the matter in the first place? The immutability of God (3:6). The flightiness of people (3:7). The desire he has for them to return. It is more than simply coming back to where he is. God wants hearts, remember, not just bodies. He wants people to feel where he is, to join him completely, to trust him wholeheartedly. The people of Malachi's day, like the kings of old, wandered from God and took up with other providers. God wants their hearts, and so he goes after their wallets. Remember, the point here is integrity, and how things fit together.

"You cannot serve both God and Money," Jesus said (Matt. 6:24). Why did he put these two together? Why not talk about some other opponent of God: sex, drugs, rock 'n' roll? Because money has a force associated with it, a pull that can be felt and loved. No doubt that money can be a force for good, a tool as useful as a garden rake. But it is very different from a carrot peeler or a jigsaw. It calls for our allegiance, and many give it. Some of these flatter themselves that their allegiance to God is no less strong, unaware of how money can seek and crush a heart.

A house we lived in had different plants on a screened-in porch. One was a small rubber tree in a plastic tub. Rubber trees require a great deal of water, and we slaked that thirst regularly, noticing how the plant thrived. We also noticed that from drainage holes near the bottom of its bucket, slender roots were emerging. Gradually, those roots grew larger, longer. Later, we saw more. Those roots were probing the concrete floor of the porch, looking for cracks that led to the ground below and the water below it. The roots of rubber trees are almost sinister in their relentless search for water. You do not, we discovered later, plant rubber trees above sewer lines or near swimming pools, since the roots will find these channels and reservoirs, encircle them, and squeeze. When we finally wised up to this plant's intentions, we moved the bucket, tearing roots that had penetrated the concrete.

Money engenders a love whose root structure spreads tendrils through a heart and disintegrates life. For this reason, it is to be handled with care. Money's inherent tendency is to distract and control. So it must be mastered, tamed.

Tithing tames money. When I give it to a person or cause other than myself, I say to money, "I'm the boss here. I use you, distribute you, make you go where I direct. I am not pushed by your insistence, neither am I at the mercy of your yearning for more. You are a tool in my hand."

Tithing teaches that money is to be a tool used by God too. So here is the best arrangement: God enables me to make money, and I, as his servant, put it back in his hands, asking him to direct its use through me. Some of his people will make a lot of money; some will barely eke out an existence. The amount of money—the number of dollars or Kruggerands or pesos or francs or yen—is irrelevant. What matters is how it is used. Withholding money because of a commitment to hoarding or out of an attempt to assist God in providing for his own is wrong. Such hoarding is no more beneficial than keeping manna an extra day. Giving it away through the tithe and offering breaks the spell and brings money back into the shed or drawer with the other tools. The love of money is the root of all evil (1 Tim. 6:10). The love of God? This yields a different plant altogether.

Serving without Enthusiasm

Malachi's recitation of charges continues as he spots those who complain, "It is futile to serve God" (3:14). They are showing their hypocrisy in the following way: They want to be among those blessed by God, but they resist carrying out his assignments. They refuse to accept the link between membership in his family and involvement with his work.

Work fits God's plan not in terms of punishment but as a means of fulfillment; in order to be most fully human, we must work.[5] The people and priests understand that work is part of God's intention,[6] but they derive no satisfaction from it: "What did we gain by carrying out his requirements?"

Vaclav Havel observes a "crisis of respect for the moral order extended to us from above." This crisis creates a condition in which "we've lost our certainty that the universe, nature, existence, our own lives are works of creation that have a definite meaning and purpose. This loss is accompanied by loss of the feeling that whatever we do must be seen in the light of a higher order of which we are part and whose authority we must respect."[7]

This "crisis of respect" is precisely what Malachi's audience manifested. They "said harsh things against" God, assuming they could do so with impunity. They found no personal benefit accruing from their labor. They concluded that "even those who challenge God escape" (3:13, 15). They disregarded the one who placed them on the earth and prepared tasks for them; they railed against the idea that God wanted them to work.

God's calling places a person and equips that person for work—for service, for ministry. Once engaged, the person then has opportunity to take delight in the particular work assigned. It is possible to complain about the task; the people and their priests were doing this and engendered God's displeasure. Better to view the labor as another of God's good gifts, another means for becoming fully what he intends. If service is seen through this lens, it can be appreciated, even enjoyed. Otherwise, work becomes drudgery.

Malachi's group seemed intent on complaint, and so they lost twice: They missed the benefit that comes when relishing what one does, and they were unable to taste God's pleasure at their accomplishment. This makes for a small and shriveled life. I contrast this with people I have met who exude enthusiasm for their labors. Three of many come to mind: a missionary translator, a contractor, and a college professor. These men passed standard retirement age without slowing; all of them found great satisfaction in their particular work. Each of them maintain and develop active, wide interests. They travel, mentor, encourage. All three are passionate about what they do; all are engaged because of their commitment to serving the Master. And these men enjoy life; their faces and their families bear testimony to that.

The Minors have made this point consistently: God wants people who will serve him well, not because they must, but because they want to. He is after people who are so in love with him that they cannot conceive of life lived in any way other than at his feet, eager to do what pleases him. In return, these people experience God's favor. Their life is not necessarily more pleasant or luxurious, but it has heft to it, presence, integrity. People such as this make a conscious decision to serve God out of gratitude and respect. They are not motivated by personal gain. Rather, they have eyes for what expands the kingdom. Because of this they are happy in their work, and what they do has significance.

Living with Integrity

Integrity occurs when the pieces of life fit together well, when there is harmony among what one says, feels, means, and does. In spiritual terms, integrity is the result of concluding that God's existence leads to his significance and from there to personal allegiance. Those who talk about God but remain locked into the service of self or money or any other force or interest cannot help but develop fissures in their souls. As one person put it, they have the worst of both worlds, missing the full joy of life with God without being able to participate fully in the alternative. Gerard Manley Hopkins commends instead a pure and winsome approach:

> Then I, why should not I love thee,
> Jesu, so much in love with me?
> Not for heaven's sake; not to be
> Out of hell by loving thee;
> Not for any gains I see;
> But just the way that thou didst me
> I do love and I will love thee:
> What must I love thee, Lord, for then?
> For being my king and God. Amen.[8]

A glassblower's shop fascinated me as a boy. I would watch enthralled as he started with single rods and a flame and then puffed and pulled and wove to form ballerinas, pianos, violins—entire orchestras. It struck me as magical. This is the work of any artist, to begin with common materials and develop complex arrangements. To fit the pieces together to fashion a larger whole. To pursue integrity.

When Solomon speaks of the "craftsman" at God's side (Prov. 8:30), he has in mind the image of an artist who takes simple dirt and forms complex humans. He is not done with the shaping but breathes into them life and then offers a means of fashioning wholeness. He wants the pieces he placed to fit. Integrity is a desired end, a worthwhile pursuit, a possible result.

If our leaders manifest integrity, then those under their care stand a chance at it, and the community will hang together reasonably well. With shoddy leadership, the community disintegrates. So let us encourage wholeness in our leaders. Let us call for competence, enjoy vulnerability, admire their good voice and hair—but let us be passionate about integrity.

And should a leader stumble, let us be full of grace. Integrity is no easy acquisition, and we need not become quickly judgmental when there are breaks or lapses. We can remember that integrity is more robust than blown glass: It can survive some jostling. It is ongoing hypocrisy we cannot condone, such as the priests around Malachi displayed. So let us encourage our leaders and prize wholeness in ourselves. Those with the prophetic voice still need to sound a warning should hypocrisy begin to creep in, while the rest will need to listen, ready to drive it away.

In the Hebrew Bible, Malachi comes immediately before Psalm 1. This arrangement, surely, is not accidental. In the opening psalm, a gauntlet is thrown: "Will you be like this?" the psalmist asks. "Will you be one who does not participate in the business of those opposed to God? Will you find your nourishment in the things of God and grow close to him?" Those who do can expect to find their lives becoming solid and whole, such that they and the communities of which they are part radiate the integrity of life in and with God.

$$\overline{10}$$

HOPE

Nahum, Zephaniah, and Zechariah

One Easter morning service at our church began with this comment from my wife:

Good morning. My name is Sue, and I'm an addict. I'm addicted to hope. I believe in happy endings, in reconciliation, in new beginnings, in good triumphing over evil.

But recently I wasn't feeling very cheery or bright. Instead, I was grieving the reality of Alzheimer's in my family. My parents are coming to visit soon, and my dad is in its middle stages. He's still coherent, yet he has a hard time finding words or remembering what's been said fifteen minutes ago. He's not that old, and this disease threatens to make his retirement meaningless. As I was thinking about their visit, I was struck with sadness. Then my sadness moved to stronger feelings: It's not fair, I thought. My parents are good people; they've given their lives to missionary work.

I've also struggled recently with feelings of loss. Friendships are drifting because of our moves, and our daughter is preparing to leave us now for college. Relatives are growing older and slowing down perceptively. My friends are experiencing loss too, and I grieve for them.

I don't like these encounters with the painful side of life. I hate to be morose. I don't like to cry. I don't like feeling out of control. I don't think I would have liked being one of Jesus' disciples on Good Friday.

What disappointment they must have felt, and what a powerful sense of loss. Three amazing years of worthwhile ministry, challenging spiritual growth, and deep relationship with the Lord crashing to an incomprehensible end. It was so unfair! What had Jesus done to deserve this?

But it didn't have to make sense to them in order to make sense for Jesus. He was involved in a story of hope, in writing an amazingly happy ending. He could see, even from the cross, being surrounded one day by millions of people full of peace and joy, with whole bodies and minds, in perfect community and delighting in the goodness of his Father.

The ironic part of the story is that none of those people deserve to be there. Fairness demands that we suffer the consequences of our disobedience. But here's the part of the story I love. God doesn't want us to get what we deserve. He wants to be gracious and merciful to us, to prove that his love for us is no empty promise.

That's why I'm addicted to hope.

Addicted to hope? As in needing it desperately, finding its coming sweet, and then craving more? The prophets would agree with this, especially since they speak so often to people beset by difficulties and disappointments. Take Nahum, for instance.

His book seems to start with the explosive rantings of an angry God: "The Lord is a jealous and avenging God; the Lord takes vengeance and is filled with wrath" (1:2). As we read more, we find that this invective is calculated. God's wrath is being directed at Nineveh, the capital of Assyria and the very town Jonah had preached to sometime earlier. Nineveh's incessant aberrant behavior has provoked him.

On the surface, it looks as though God is lashing out with the anger that so many say is typical—and the reason for their disinterest in him. Some probing of the text, however, might alter that perception. Consider the way Nahum blends talk of God's impending judgment with assertions of his long-standing patience and mercy, for instance, so that he becomes "a refuge in times of trouble" (1:7).

Then there is the craft with which Nahum describes God. In Hebrew, the opening eight verses of this first chapter form an acrostic, as Nahum carefully begins each new sentence with a new letter of the Hebrew alphabet. A similar thing happens in Psalm 119, where the acrostic is sustained much longer. The form tells us something about content in both places. For Nahum, this poetic presentation shows that God's wrath is not the petulant act of a miffed deity but the studied, careful response of a long-suffering Majesty. God's wrath resembles an episode in Jesus' life, when he cleared the temple of money changers ensconced there.

Jesus appears on that occasion to be passionately upset, about to vent his divine spleen against the hypocrites and mercenaries gathered in the holy place. We are ready to grant him that privilege, because we would have been angry too. But John remembers that Jesus paused to plait a whip of cords before going in (John 2:15). He did not grab the first blunt instrument that came to hand but stopped to weave an implement. The outburst of an angry man or the calculated action of one about to make an important point? His action, like Nahum's careful poetry, suggests intentionality and not irrational anger.

"The Lord," who, as Nahum affirms, "is slow to anger" (1:3), is not merely pitching a fit. He is a focused, even tender, Father who must finally bring punishment to children who are unashamedly rebellious. Nahum even implies this with his preferred name for God. He uses *Yahweh* in Hebrew ("the Lord" in English), which tends to be more personal. Many names could have expressed God's coming in power—the Lord of Hosts, for instance—but Nahum selects one that conveys a warmer tone.

God's eyes range throughout the entire world. He can reduce a past world power such as Egypt's Thebes (3:8–10) and can deal with the current dominant force in similar ways. Geographic and political borders are irrelevant on the day of the Lord; he will judge the entire world. He is powerful; what he says he will do will take place. His promise of restoration (2:2) is not empty campaign rhetoric.

Prophets such as Nahum do not write simply to announce that God is about to crush the enemy. They affirm that God is aware of what is going on, available for help now, and certain about what lies ahead. With good news they lift the heads of those who are weighed down by aggravating circumstance and long-standing oppression. Hope grows in an environment such as this.

The True Meaning of Hope

Tragically, *hope* is a weak word these days, meaning little more than what we feel when it's time for a job review, or when the Yorkshire pudding is about to come out of the oven, or when we're searching for a parking spot at the mall. This is probably why the prophets confuse the denizens of suburbia: Their message just does not seem to fit with those who face little active trouble for their faith or who are busy with careers, relationships, and hobbies.

But turn the prophets loose in parts of the world where the people of God are at the business end of rifles, whips, clubs, and brands. Rattle their words around in minds innately suspicious of the status quo. What of the one who has just learned of cancer in his child, or whose parent has developed a wasting disease, or whose job has abruptly and callously been terminated? What about those whose prospects are bleak on account of past generations' rapacious appetites? Travel to parts of East Africa, India, or China, where believers are routinely tortured, enslaved, or killed. When physical troubles and spiritual attacks stack up like cord wood, what does hope mean then?

Hope sustains you in the welter of struggles that scurry through the heart and mind like tadpoles in a pond.[1] It draws you into the new day and carries you through the many interminable ones that follow. It staves off depression and anger and gives energy for carrying on.

We think of the prophets as writing about the future, and they do. But their interest resides less with helping us chart events in a nice, neat way than with assisting us through the minefields inherent to life lived for and with God. They assure us that God is sufficient for what we are going through now and for what is likely to smack us later. They persist in saying that the one we cling to is deserving of our trust, that hope in God is legitimate and beneficial. Seers such as Nahum give us, as they gave beleaguered Jews surrounded by numerous foes and detractors, reason to press on.

Carried by the Spirit to a time still distant, they bring back reports: Foes will fall, God will triumph, the planet's equilibrium will be restored. Their messages instill hope for the inevitably trying days ahead. With their wonderful dreams and tales of better times, they offer a vision of life far different from current experience. Prophets see what is not as though it actually were and invite others to adopt their perspective despite current evidence to the contrary. They offer hope, but they do so by way of a challenge: Believe that a power as awesome and far-reaching as Assyria's will one day soon be little more than rubble, and you are likely to believe anything. Exactly.

Hope Sustains

Zephaniah joins Nahum as a second witness against Assyria, promising that God will "stretch out his hand . . . leaving Nineveh utterly desolate" (2:13). Remarkable, that God would focus so much on Assyria. He sent Jonah to preach for their repentance and then Nahum and Zephaniah to condemn them for not making good on the confession sparked by that earlier messenger. Peter would assess much later a similar situation involving different people, who, like the Assyrians, were guilty of turning away from the one they had claimed to follow: "It would have been better for them not to have known the way of righteousness, than to have known it and then to turn their backs on the sacred command that was passed on to them" (2 Peter 2:21).

The Lord's obvious interest in Assyria indicates that he had ample room for them in his kingdom; in the words of other messengers, the good news of God's love was meant to occasion great joy for "all the people" (Luke 2:10). Assyria demurs, as do the others nations, such as Philistia, Moab, Ammon, and Cush, that fall under Zephaniah's broad message of coming destruction. Judah's inhabitants are stirred into this batch too, "oppressors, rebellious and defiled" (3:1), who "turn back from following the LORD, and neither seek the LORD nor inquire of him" (1:6).

Zephaniah's contemporaries were seers who gave false hope (3:4). God sends him to those tangled by the snares of despair and indifference with a message rooted in reality. Few would have listened to or liked what they heard: Present trouble was simply too real, the power of Assyria too great. The perception of God was that of a remote deity, too far gone to be of any assistance or threat, and so his emissaries were viewed with suspicion.

And yet, through this prophet God draws near. He spins a story of destruction for the cruel oppressors, of deliverance for the keepers of faith. A "remnant" will plunder the marauder (2:9); long-term foes will fade into oblivion. The scattered will be gathered, and the displaced will soon be home (3:19–20).

It is a compelling story, the stuff of dreams—and visions—for those willing to hope. Sadly, most were not. Less than sixty years after Zephaniah and Nahum, Judah goes into exile herself, as a consequence for hard hearts. Ironically, this happened shortly after the Babylonians overthrew Assyria, in fulfillment of the prophets' predictions.

Walter Brueggemann suggests that there are two key temptations during an exile: assimilation and despair.[2] On the one hand is the inclination toward becoming like the inhabitants of the host country, adopting their speech, customs, and even religion. On the other is the slide toward the hopelessness of ever seeing the home fires burn again. In both cases, God becomes incidental, if not downright culpable.

As an exile in Babylon, you would be surrounded by people resentful of their fate. You would witness cruelties; you might experience them yourself. Your children might be drifting, especially if they entered captivity young. Having grown up in this environment, they might be talking about settling in this new land, making the best of a crummy situation. They speak in hushed whispers when you are around, about the newest Babylonian mantel pieces. How would you deal with the exile?

You might pop on a wig of red, curly hair, stick out your chin, grin, and say, "The sun'll come out tomorrow." Maybe you prefer a Pollyanna blond, complete with an extra-large gleaming smile. Or you're a brunette beneath the bed covers, clutching your little schnauzer as you suddenly realize that the terrible darkness you just experienced was only a dream. "There's no place like home," you announce cheerfully to your friends.

That bubble bursts with the reality that home is Babylon; this is no dream. It is light-years from where you grew up and a daily reminder of how far your people have wandered from God. What will sustain you here?

Annie Dillard asked a group of aspiring writers, "How many of you will give your life to this craft?" Every hand in the room shot high. In her heart, she was more skeptical. She tried to convey what the writing life requires: "You can't be anything else. You must go at your life with a broadax."[3] To cut away everything other than what you will need to write: How many would make this sacrifice? But without it, writing is only a hobby, a way to fill or kill time. It is diversion, not life.

It was very grim, this time far from home. So the prophets come, even during the exile, to speak of life with God. To follow God: How many will give themselves to this? Pause before answering. Because a yes means discarding the accrued baggage of misperceptions, bad habits, and harmful addictions only to travel a road full of twists and turns. The journey is treacherous, uncertain, alternatively delightful and worrisome. Time passes, and progress is measured in blood.

What will sustain you on this journey? In a word, it is hope. In God's calculus, "suffering produces perseverance; perseverance, character; and character, hope" (Rom. 5:3–4). Hope grows in the crucible of adversity, when God steers us into the storm and then hands over the tiller.

Zechariah, a child of the exile, walks out of Babylon carrying the same tune, another messenger of hope.

Put Your Hope in God

As Babylon trampled Assyria, so Persia decimates Babylon. Then Cyrus, the leader of Persia, with a sweeping humanitarian gesture, permits Jews to return home. God moves hearts in response (Ezra 1:5), and many walk back. Zechariah is there, along with the prophet Haggai. Together they pitch in with clearing rubble, mixing mud, and laying block for a new temple. Zechariah, assured by God (Zech. 1:16), knows this temple will go up. Others are less confident. They are pestered by opposition and morose when comparing this temple to the previous one (Ezra 3:12; Hag. 2:3). Could God really be in this project?

It's a test, hard on the heels of the exile, which had been another test. The prophet remains steady, tethered to God's promise: "Just as I had determined to bring disaster upon you and showed no pity when your fathers angered me, . . . so now I have determined to do good again to Jerusalem and Judah" (8:14–15).

When will that be? Trouble continues to swarm like bees. Local officials are hassling the building project, Persia has a standing army nearby, and the people are a few handfuls of minutes from revolting against their leadership. How soon before God embarks on his good work?

It hardly matters. Zechariah's heart is captivated by hope that lifts him above the immediate difficulties into the coming glory. There is a king on the horizon, and beside him, all else pales (9:9–11). The Lord will appear, the Sovereign will march, God will save (9:14, 16). Zechariah says all this with confidence, certain of an outcome that seems unlikely in the face of current circumstances. This is hope speaking, unfettered by the chains of despair and free from the entanglements of assimilation.

We are easily snared by both. We develop fluency in the local culture and language with surprising ease. Or we sink deep in the mud of loneliness and pessimism. We do not realize how desperate we are for a prophet. We become like those Antoine de Saint-Exupéry notices "beneath the dismal winter sky of Toulouse" during his stint as a pilot with the mail service. He is riding a bus to his plane one morning, one passenger among many worn, old clerks on their way to an office. "Suddenly," he says, "I had a vision of the face of destiny":

> Old bureaucrat, my comrade, it is not you who are to blame. No one ever helped you escape. You, like a termite, built your peace by blocking up with cement every chink and cranny through which the light might pierce. You rolled yourself up into a ball in your genteel security, raising a modest rampart against the winds and the tides and the stars. You have chosen not to be perturbed by great problems, having trouble enough to forget your own fate as man. You are not the dweller upon an errant planet and do not ask yourself questions to which there are no answers. You are a petty bourgeois of Toulouse. Nobody grasped you by the shoulder while there was still time.[4]

Prophets such as Zechariah cannot stand idly by while others move through their days indifferent to God. They seize people by the shoulders and shake: "Do not become entwined. Do not give way to despair," they say. Put your hope in God. When you do this, you will notice changes in a previously barren life.[5] You will see the King. You will draw hope from him, set hope upon him.

A Language of Hope

A quick parenthesis for two points about Zechariah. First, the book is widely used for work on "eschatology," the study of the end times. Prophets generally are consulted when thoughts turn to the future, and Zechariah, along with Daniel and Revelation, has a distinctive quality that makes it a candidate for special handling. The problem is that fascination with things pertaining to the end can obscure other lessons these books have to teach. We busily mine the prophets to build a timetable for the Lord's second advent, but we give less energy to pondering why his coming back is of interest or what its inevitability implies for us now.

Confusion about eschatology, along with the skirmishes different interpretations touch off, discourages saints and repels those investigating the faith. It would be better for us to fashion ways of understanding texts and interacting with one another that honor the Spirit's intention, preserve peace within the community, and manifest ongoing winsomeness for those who are searching. It is worth remembering that while believers are not necessarily linked by similar interpretations or experience, they do anticipate the same destination; this hope is one point all who follow Jesus have in common.

The second point concerns the unusual writing style of Zechariah. In literary terms, it includes a chunk called "apocalyptic" (1:7–6:15), a genre found in parts of Daniel, much of Revelation, and many noncanonical "prophets." Apocalyptic writing regularly includes fantastic images and sweeping battles as the spiritual and physical worlds intersect and collide. Often angelic messengers interpret portions of the visions that routinely fill these writings, which are more concerned with the broad sweep of good's victory over evil than with particular applications of moral imperatives.

Think of such writings as the underground literature of a people suffering occupation by a foreign power. Using an elaborate code, apocalyptic writing tells a plain story: As real and onerous as the current threat might be, God will triumph in the end. Along the way battles will be fought in heaven, on earth, and in between. They will be fierce; people will be wounded and die. But the outcome is certain: God will win the war. He is strong enough to ensure this outcome and generous enough to include people in its blessings.

Writing such as this requires a reader's active attention. One might quibble about how to interpret various symbols, but there is no question about what is at stake. In the world of apocalyptic literature, there is no room for the "petty bourgeois" dozing fitfully in a bus that rumbles along quiet streets under heavy clouds. A war is on, and lives hang in the balance. On which side will you fall? And what will see you through the next battle?

Apocalyptic writing uses the language of triumph and speaks from the perspective of hope realized. It is news from the other side telegraphed back to those still entrenched, reporting a victory for the people of God. This is why it makes sense for such writing to emerge from those who count God as their Lord but who still face gray dawns. For these, fixing hope on God is precisely right—counterintuitive, but right. In the face of whatever slings and arrows life hurls, in hope they travel "higher up and deeper in,"[6] ever nearing God.

Hope Enables Us to Press On

The Smithsonian's Museum of Natural History is chock full of stuff; one can easily spend a day there seeing only a fraction of its many displays. One section should not be missed, however. On the second floor, high above the mastodon dominating the central lobby, there is a collection of gemstones and minerals. These stones are set in hammered, cast, and ornately carved metals, arrayed in a mesmerizing cascade of crystalline rainbows, or nestled beneath printed descriptions.

The showpiece of the exhibit is the fabled Hope diamond, forty-five carats of dazzling grayish-blue rock the size of a carpenter's thumb. It arrived at the Smithsonian in 1958 as a gift donated by the firm of Harry Winston, Inc. In a space dedicated to precious stones, this one has pride of place, suspended in a transparent cylinder that can be viewed from all sides. It is a brilliant, hard, beautiful, valuable gem. People form a line without complaint to walk around the Hope diamond, quietly, almost reverently. They linger near its dais, drawn by its magnificence. A postcard featuring this stone sells briskly at the museum's gift shop.

Hope is such a gem, laid into a heart by God with special care. This gift shines; it is resilient, lovely, valuable. It is meant to be appreciated and enjoyed and ought to evoke a gasp. It is supposed to take your breath away—that God would entrust us with such a thing, that it would be part of his plan for us.

"Those who hope in the LORD will renew their strength. They will soar on wings like eagles; they will run and not grow weary, they will walk and not be faint" (Isa. 40:31). Hope is God's gift that enables us to press on through persecution and disappointment (1 Thess. 1:3). Because of hope, we can also encourage others as together we push out frontiers.

I was loaned a collection of stories about famous explorers, arranged according to the continents they investigated. The South

Pole group, led by Sir Robert Scott, caught my eye. Scott mounted the first modern attempt at the pole and, in 1904, failed to find it. In 1909, Ernest Shackleton, a member of Scott's earlier team, came within 112 miles of the elusive ninety-degree mark before being forced to turn back. Three years later, Roald Amundsen succeeded. His team set up a tent and lashed a second stick, bearing a Norwegian flag, to its main pole. The victors gave speeches and smoked cigars in a circle formed by measuring instruments before heading back in dogsleds. They beat Robert Scott's second hunt for the South Pole by thirty-seven days. Scott's group, stripped of provisions and scoured by the weather as they slogged back to their base after seeing Amundsen's tent and flag, all perished on the Antarctic ice cap.

There is in the human spirit an urge to push out the frontier—in medicine, art, science, geography, and more. It's what Sir Peter Scott, Robert's son, calls the "excitement of discovery."[7] Edmund Hilary, who climbed to the top of the world in 1953, put it more poetically. He tackled Mount Everest "because it was there."

In spiritual terms, we call that hope, which propels us *there*, away from *here*, out into the wild blue yonder. Robert Scott went, twice, far from here, determined to get there. He spent his life on this pursuit, shedding gear along the way in an attempt to lighten the load and make success a possibility. My book repeats some of Scott's final words in a letter to a friend, left to be found by others: "We are pegging out in a very comfortless spot. . . . We are in a desperate state, feet frozen, etc. No fuel and a long way from food, but it would do your heart good to be in our tent, to hear our songs and the cheery conversation." To the end his British upper lip remained stiff, and he died near a point measurable only by instruments. On his marker in Antarctica is etched a line from Tennyson's *Ulysses:* "to strive, to seek, to find, and not to yield."[8]

Tucked into this borrowed book to mark my place was another letter, written eighty-three years after Scott froze and starved to death. On the surface, this letter offers its own songs and cheery conversation: The writer's children run barefoot around the homestead, and house projects are squeezed in between other responsibilities. The letter is written on a yellow aerogram; the stamps bear a language most do not read. Its brief paragraphs tell not only of domestic but of church life: There are squabbles brewing among young leaders; there is pressure from detractors who do not like Christians.

This letter's author is an explorer, part of a couple who whacked into the bush years ago. The profession for which both trained long and hard is only tangentially used anymore; now time is filled with raising kids, fashioning means to cope with limited electricity and water, repairing broken things, teaching others how to raise new crops, showing Jesus. They were hurled by hope far from the secure here, and their faces point only one way.

Hope such as this infects others too. The letter tells of an evangelist encouraged by this couple who is learning the language of another tribe. He goes every Saturday with several from the church to different outlying villages; another group of ten believers stays at the church and prays for the travelers. Residents of a village report on the impact of this evangelist: "When we first heard this story of Jesus translated from another tongue, it was just the voice of man. But now we hear it in our own language first—it must be from God!" Exciting, huh? the writer asks. Never easy, often dangerous. But exciting! So ends this letter.

Hope presses you toward new frontiers or pulls you there. Living on these edges requires courage, dedication, strength; one does not cross the line without them. Hope lifts your eyes to look out past the rim of normal vision. And you must go, for your own sake and the sake of those you love.

Frontiers can lay near the equator or ninety degrees from it or somewhere in between. They crop up in the office, warehouse, and classroom. They stretch out in relationships, with people and God. There are frontiers awaiting those willing to push past the comfortable approaches to ecology and economics. Will you cross the line for a journey over the ice? Will you strip down as did Scott and leave your gear in the snow so that you can reach your destination? Will you take a broadax to your life, not merely so that you can plant a flag where no person's foot has ever fallen but so that you can take up permanent residence outside the comfort zone, where you are likely to die?

Hope will help. Hope hangs like a full moon, shiny as a lighthouse, directing your steps toward the destination you seek. Hope is within you, lodged there by God as bright and broad as a thumb-sized diamond, reminding you of what he has done and is still doing. Hope wafts around you, pungent as burning pine, filling the air of the realm you inhabit if you are a follower of Jesus.

Prisoners of Hope

Zechariah speaks about "prisoners of hope" (9:12), and the image disturbs with its dissonance. Surely hope frees us, right? Yes and no. By the Giver of hope we are freed to enter a new life, but we cannot move far from hope with any success or joy—and so we are its prisoner. A prisoner of hope: It's a little like being a victim of wedlock. Locked by marriage to the one we love is no punishment, no task grimly borne. In love we gladly bind our self to another. In hope we are similarly imprisoned and thus free to live fully.

If only for this life we have hope, we are desperate creatures. This is the opinion of Paul (1 Cor. 15:19), a man acquainted with prisons. Though often chained, Paul rarely seemed bound; his letters reflect a busy and focused mind. He could not take his body far, so he roamed along other frontiers, exploring. He did not lose heart, because he never lost sight of hope.

On that Easter Sunday, as we looked out over a beautiful valley toward a mountain, Sue concluded this way:

> I'm addicted to hope. It doesn't mean I don't get sad, don't struggle. I'm not looking forward to having my family change as my kids go off to college and their own lives. I don't relish losing good friends. And I am not through grieving the difficulties my parents will face with the challenges of a debilitating illness.
>
> But Easter reminds me, proves to me, that God is good, that God is love, that he will ultimately win. One day my dad will have a new body, as Jesus did on Easter morning. His mind will be clear, and with that clear mind I know he'll be praising God with everything that's in him. And I know that one day I'll be together with friends and family, enjoying relationships deeper than anything I've had on earth. And there won't be a place for tears, because God will wipe them all from our eyes.

Prisoners and addicts—strange words to be associated with something so wonderful as hope. But we are people with intense needs, which must be matched by potent cures. Hope entices us to entrust ourselves to God's care. It encourages us to anticipate his victory. Hope flings the good news skyward like a rocket, fills the air we breathe with it. "The gospel, in our moment of exhaustion, is a caring promise and a wondrous assertion that we belong and are intensely cared for."[9]

"The LORD your God is with you, he is mighty to save. He will take great delight in you, he will quiet you with his love, he will rejoice over you with singing" (Zeph. 3:17). Zephaniah's blending of present and future is for all who face the threats of despair and assimilation from an exile. The former makes us brittle; the latter makes us spongy. Neither prepares us for long-term living. Those with hope can depend instead on "the power of an indestructible life" (Heb. 7:16, 19). Like Jesus, they can face what comes without perturbation because no thing can rob them of what is most precious. The rains may pelt, the streams may rise, the wind may howl and batter all in its way, but this life does not fall, because its foundation is securely tied to hope.

Hope anchors a life lashed by despair and assimilation. It energizes us, enabling us to push out frontiers. It finds toeholds from which to climb or spring. Consider the Lord's model prayer, in which the stately almost benign "thy kingdom come" becomes understood more accurately as a war cry bellowed by the prisoners of hope: "Bring on your kingdom!" Those who hope call this out with feeling and meaning, because they see what God is doing, can do, will do. The cry launches them into a life that will throw them forcefully back in their seats as they lift off.

In a word, what we need for this life—for stability and progress—is hope. And in a word, this hope, according to Scripture, is best understood in terms of Jesus. His presence makes the difference in a heart; his work ensures a bright future; his desires fuel the obedience that influences those around the people in whom he dwells. When we, for instance, call the people of faith as well as those who still need God to "seek the LORD" (Zeph. 2:3), we help to change the course of their lives. When we steer by the star of a celebration being prepared by the Lord for his own (Zech. 14:16), our own hearts grow glad.

The prophets anticipate Jesus; he is "the hope of Israel" (Acts 28:20) to which they point when they speak of a coming day when God will enter human history noticeably. Their vision encompasses two entries: One we have experienced already; another is yet to come. Both are meant to effect change among and through those who face troubled days. With hope, one can move toward the roiled river that leads to the tossing sea. A day is coming when all will be right. So for now, take a deep breath and dive in.

NOTES

Introduction

1. The adjective was probably intended to describe the length of these books, even though Hosea and Zechariah are both longer than the "major" prophet Daniel, but the moniker is unfortunate. Who cares about "minor" league baseball? Aren't the "minor" points of arguments negligible? Don't serious actors shun "minor" roles? Doesn't society restrict the rights and privileges of "minors"? Perhaps it is time for a new label.

Chapter 1

1. "New" is a relative term. For example, if I take my daughter to Chile for a visit and there on a fine Sunday afternoon in Santiago we go to Los Dominicos, where she eats an *empanada*, she has done something new. But it is new only for her. People in Santiago have been eating *empanadas* at Los Dominicos (and for good reason) for years.

2. Perhaps Jonah had done such a good job of rationalizing his behavior that he was drugged by self-deception. It is also possible that the sleep was God-induced and used by God to help Jonah come to grips with the severity of his situation. Prophets often received messages in their sleep (Dan. 8:18 is one example), and this slumber may have helped Jonah reach the conclusion he mentions in 1:12.

3. William Willimon makes startling observations such as this; I am indebted to his books, such as *The Intrusive Word* (Grand Rapids: Eerdmans, 1994).

4. J. B. Phillips's book, *Your God Is Too Small* (New York: Macmillan, 1997), is slim, but the ideas it contains expand rapidly once the cover opens.

Chapter 2

1. F. F. Bruce calls Habakkuk a temple prophet and finds a likely job description in 1 Chronicles 25:1. Bruce also notices how few of the Minor Prophets are directly identified as prophets. T. E. McComiskey, ed., *The Minor Prophets* (Grand Rapids: Baker, 1993), 832.

2. This phrase occurs three times in the New Testament, more than any Old Testament passage other than Psalm 110. F. F. Bruce even suggests that Paul wrote Romans as an explication of Habakkuk 2:4 (F. F. Bruce, *Hebrews,* New International Commentary on the New Testament [Grand Rapids: Eerdmans 1964], 274).

3. A book with this title, written by a son of Taylor's, can easily be acquired. Buy it. Read it.

Chapter 3

1. No one knows exactly when this was. Some scholars date the book at 800 B.C., while others prefer the 600s B.C.

2. The translation comes from Gerald Hawthorne, *Philippians* (Dallas: Word, 1983), 75.

3. Weil's chapter on "decreation" comes in the collection of her writings compiled by George A. Panichas (*The Simone Weil Reader* [New York: David McKay Company, 1981], 350–56).

4. Ibid., 356.

5. Weil quotes Augustine: "He who created us without our help will not save us without our consent" (ibid., 355).

6. Both characters are from Dorothy Sayers, whose detective series featuring them continues to enthrall readers.

7. This is Nevill Coghill's translation of Chaucer's *Prologue* (New York: Penguin Books, 1951), 9.

8. Or the household of Stephanas (1 Cor. 1:16), Caesar (Phil. 4:22), or Onesiphorus (2 Tim. 1:16).

9. Joel Stein, speaking of hockey legend Wayne Gretzky, notes "how awesomely subtle greatness can be" (*Time*, 26 April 1999, 114).

Chapter 4

1. A portion of this section makes an annual appearance each Advent. Typically, Christmas pageants quote the reference to a coming One from Bethlehem but neglect the larger context of this prophecy.

2. It is good to remember that Jesus asked for different things from different people. For example, he asked James and John to leave their family business on his behalf (Mark 1:19–20).

3. Like the women of means who funded his campaigns (see Luke 8:3).

4. The last letter John Wesley wrote was to William Wilberforce. In it, Wesley says, "Unless God has raised you up for this very thing, you will be worn out by the opposition of men and devils. But if God be for you, who can be against you? Are all of them together stronger than God? O be not weary of well doing! Go on, in the name of God and in the power of his might, till even American slavery (the vilest that ever saw the sun) shall vanish away before it." This letter is quoted in many sources.

5. From Christopher Hancock, "The Shrimp Who Stopped Slavery," *Christian History* 16, no. 1 (1997): 12.

6. Hancock refers to Wilberforce's fierce resolve: "So enormous, so dreadful, so irremediable did the trade's wickedness appear that my own mind was completely made up for abolition. Let the consequences be what they would; I from this time determined that I would never rest until I had effected its abolition" (ibid.).

7. A character of Madeleine L'Engle's quotes the fourteenth-century British poet William Langland: "But all the wickedness in the world which man may do or think is no more to the mercy of God than a live coal dropped into the sea" (*A Live Coal in the Sea* [San Francisco: HarperSanFrancisco, 1997], 167).

8. "The one who judges us most finally will be the one who loves us most fully." So Frederick Buechner's winsome theological dictionary, *Wishful Thinking* (New York: Harper & Row, 1973), defines mercy in the entry dealing with judgment. James adds that "mercy triumphs over judgment" (James 2:13).

9. Psalm 103:10. You can almost see the smile spreading on David's face as he draws this conclusion. The Hebrew term *chesed* appears twice around this verse (vv. 8, 11). David knows well the personal impact of divine mercy.

10. George Stulac points out the textual difficulties with James 4:6 and concludes that the evidence favors a translation that emphasizes God's longing for people devoted to him (Stulac, *James* [Downers Grove, Ill.: InterVarsity Press, 1993], 146f.).

Chapter 5

1.Walter Brueggemann traces these historical developments in *Cadences of Home* (Louisville: Westminster John Knox Press, 1977), 99–134.

2. Seasons of quiet are available through a service such as Intermission, offered by Cedar Ridge Community Church in suburban Maryland. Intermission gathers people for contemplative reflection and worship so as, in the words of their literature, to "affirm and nurture the image of God in everyone and to be woven into the fabric of communities of faith across cultures and throughout the ages . . . embracing with reverence the beauty and mystery of God's romance with the soul."

3. The actual Hebrew word is *Sabaoth,* which appears in Martin Luther's hymn "A Mighty Fortress."

4. Joe Stowell turns a phrase nicely when he describes the privilege of proximity as "an adoring dependence on the One who will not leave us alone" (*Far from Home* [Chicago: Moody Press, 1998], 29).

5. One of Judaism's fundamental dictums was "Be holy, because I [that is, God] am holy" (Lev. 11:44–45).

6. Libertines are those who adopted the attitude of "anything goes." In modern North American culture, their watchword would be "whatever."

7. Paul sharpens this point in Galatians 3:24: "The law was put in charge to lead us to Christ that we might be justified by faith." Paul's Greek uses the image of a tutor employed by a householder for the purpose of educating young children. Once that task has been accomplished, the teacher is dismissed with thanks.

8. "Once we have understood we are nothing, the object of all our efforts is to become nothing. It is for this that we suffer with resignation, it is for this that we act, it is for this that we pray" (Weil, "Decreation," in *The Simone Weil Reader,* ed. George Panichas [New York: David McKay Company, 1981], 352f.).

Chapter 6

1. Jon Krakauer's compelling *Into Thin Air* (New York: Doubleday, 1998) illustrates a number of powerful lessons.

2. Amos provides sufficient data for dating his ministry in the first half of the eighth century B.C. To put this in perspective, this would put Amos roughly 200 years after David and 350 years before the close of the Old Testament canon.

3. Bethel got its start as a religious center from Jacob, who commemorated an encounter with God there by building a small altar. Eventually, that altar became a must-see site, attracting visitors, then business, then an institution. The move from interesting place to competition with Jerusalem to holy site for true worshipers has been repeated often in our day but is equally wrongheaded in any age.

4. This is another of those recurring patterns in Scripture: Those called to serve the Lord regularly are thrown into difficult situations. Look, for example, at Acts 9:16.

5. It is interesting to notice that several Old Testament laws are tied directly to fear. That is, the basis for the behavior called for by a law is one's fear of God. See

Leviticus 19:14, 32; 25:17, 36, 43. Paul (and more on Paul below) makes a similar but more wide-reaching point in 2 Corinthians 7:1.

6. Polycarp's story is told with more detail in Michael Holmes, *The Apostolic Fathers* (Grand Rapids: Baker, 1989). Nate Saint's tale is recounted most recently by his son Steve Nate in Susan Bergman, ed., *Martyrs: Contemporary Writers on Modern Lives of Faith* (San Francisco: Harper, 1996).

7. Ezekiel speaks for many when he repeats God's words: "For I take no pleasure in the death of anyone. . . . Repent and live!" (Ezek. 18:32).

8. Pascal's *Pensees* is available in many editions. This quote comes from Honor Levi's translation for the World Classics (Oxford: Oxford University Press, 1995), 141. In a different phrasing but with a similar sense, Mary praises the "Mighty One [who] has done great things" and whose "mercy extends to those who fear him, from generation to generation" (see Luke 1:49–50).

9. This is the point the apostle John makes in places such as these: "[The angel] said in a loud voice, 'Fear God and give him glory'" (Rev. 14:7); "Those who had been victorious over the beast . . . sang, . . . 'Who will not fear you, O Lord?'" (Rev. 15:2, 4); "Then a voice came from the throne, saying: 'Praise our God, all you his servants, you who fear him, both small and great!'" (Rev. 19:5).

10. Once again we can learn from John, who knows that "perfect love drives out fear" (1 John 4:18). It might also be apt to say that perfect fear drives out fear as well.

Chapter 7

1. One observer, describing this method for handling conflict, found a useful analogy in a kitchen appliance: "Know what happens when you put twenty pounds of garbage in a trash compactor? You still have twenty pounds of garbage."

2. Noelle Oxenhandler, "The Lost While," in *How We Want to Live,* ed. Susan Shreve and Porter Shreve (Boston: Beacon Press, 1998), 95.

3. It is likely that Hosea was relatively young when he began, since his ministry spanned a rule of kings who reigned for more than sixty years.

4. This is Eugene Peterson's image from "Lashed to the Mast," *Leadership* 7, no. 3 (1986): 52.

5. The writer of Hebrews applies Psalm 40:8 to Jesus: "Here I am—it is written about me in the scroll—I have come to do your will, O God" (Heb. 10:7).

6. Contemporary macho wisdom updates Nietzsche to say, "What doesn't kill you makes you stronger." This misguided sentiment pulls the emphasis away from how God helps and what he wants us to learn. James counsels patience in the midst of adversity and says that trouble makes us strong by linking us to God (James 4:7–11).

7. This gripping story is told in Raymond Davis, *Fire on the Mountains* (Grand Rapids: Zondervan, 1966).

8. Ibid., 214–18.

9. Paul issues that pesky, inconvenient reminder that love "always hopes" (1 Cor. 13:7).

Chapter 8

1. This isn't quite right. We have two suggestive names: Pethuel ("open to God") and Joel ("God is God").

2. From *A Christmas Carol,* part of an old, undated copy of *Christmas Books* (London: Chapman & Hall), 16.

3. John Piper quotes from Müeller's autobiography in his thought-provoking *Desiring God* (Sisters, Ore.: Multnomah, 1996), 132. Piper has been a contemporary champion of the "happy" life, and for this contribution we can be grateful.

4. It helps to think of the prophetic "day of the Lord" as an epoch more than as a span of twenty-four hours. The day begins with the Messiah's arrival, includes God's great judgment, and tapers off into a season—a very long season—of reward for life's actions and decisions.

5. A. L. Clements, ed., *John Donne's Poetry* (New York: W. W. Norton, 1966), 87.

Chapter 9

1. Douglas Coupland, *Life after God* (New York: Simon & Schuster, 1994), 273.

2. "Revere" combines a prefix for repetition with the Latin *vereri*, which translates as "be in awe of, fear."

3. To this day, the "most formal" name of God is still pronounced during public reading of the Scriptures by using the far more common "Adonai" when the Hebrew tetragrammaton *YHWH* is encountered in the text. In ancient times, scribes would pause to wash their hands before and after writing this name.

4. Dallas Willard translates the phrase "hallowed be your name" as "may Your name be treasured and loved" (*Divine Conspiracy* [San Francisco: Harper, 1998], 269).

5. Peter Drucker draws from his considerable study of business mechanisms and applications the conclusion that one of humanity's fundamental needs is to be engaged in work that means something. He raises this point often. Tim Stafford, writing in *Christianity Today* (15 November 1999), 46, says that in Drucker's view, "the best thing you can offer a person is the chance to contribute to a worthwhile cause."

6. Work is not the result of God's early curse for sin in the Garden but a part of his plan. See Genesis 1:28; 2:15; and Ephesians 2:10.

7. Vaclav Havel, "The Divine Revolution," *Utne Reader* (July/August 1998): 57.

8. This is the latter half of Hopkins's "O Deus, ego amo te," from W. H. Gardner and N. H. MacKenzie, eds., *The Poems of Gerard Manley Hopkins* (Oxford: Oxford University Press, 1967), 213.

Chapter 10

1. "The origin of hope is hurt," according to Walter Brueggemann. He makes this unexpected but astute observation in *Old Testament Theology,* ed. Patrick D. Miller (Minneapolis: Fortress Press, 1992), 50.

2. Brueggemann's *Cadences of Home* offers fascinating insight into the exigencies and implications of the Jewish exile (Louisville: John Knox Press, 1997), 115–17.

3. From *The Annie Dillard Reader* (New York: HarperCollins, 1994), 429. This exchange occurs in her essay "Holy the Firm."

4. Antoine de Saint-Exupéry, *Wind, Sand and Stars* (New York: Harcourt, Brace & Company, 1940), 11.

5. Psalms 126 and 147 illustrate this point nicely.

6. This is C. S. Lewis's phrase. It describes where the High King and his court are heading in the final volume of his Narnia Chronicles.

7. In April 1987, *The National Geographic* ran articles about follow-up trips to Antarctica's pole. Peter Scott offered "expert commentary" on one expedition.

8. Ibid., 555.

9. Brueggemann, *Cadences of Home,* 134.

Dan Schmidt studied at Wheaton College, Trinity Evangelical Divinity School, Princeton Theological Seminary, and Hebrew Union College (Cincinnati). He is the author of *Follow the Leader* (Victor Books) and articles for newspapers and magazines. He currently pastors an international church near San Jose, Costa Rica, where he lives with his wife and daughters.